MOCTEZUMA'S REVENGE

*Eight Navajos and a Teacher
Explore the Mysteries of Ancient Aztlán*

MOCTEZUMA'S REVENGE

Eight Navajos and a Teacher
Explore the Mysteries of Ancient Aztlán

Andrew Shows

© 2025 by Andrew Shows
All Rights Reserved
No part of this book may be reproduced in any form or by any electronic or mechanical means including information storage and retrieval systems without permission in writing from the publisher, except by a reviewer who may quote brief passages in a review.

Sunstone books may be purchased for educational, business, or sales promotional use. For information please write: Special Markets Department, Sunstone Press, P.O. Box 2321, Santa Fe, New Mexico 87504-2321.
Printed on acid-free paper
∞
eBook: 978-1-61139-781-9

Library of Congress Cataloging-in-Publication Data

Names: Shows, Andrew, 1951- author
Title: Moctezuma's revenge : eight Navajos and a teacher explore the mysteries of ancient Aztlán / Andrew Shows.
Description: Santa Fe : Sunstone Press, [2025] | Summary: "This book narrates an adventure in Mexico of eight Navajo students and their teacher through unbelievable but true experiences in 1975"-- Provided by publisher.
Identifiers: LCCN 2025036699 | ISBN 9781632937667 paperback | ISBN 9781632937674 hardcover | ISBN 9781611397819 epub
Subjects: LCSH: Aztlán--Description and travel | Mexico--Description and travel
Classification: LCC F1216.5 .S56 2025 | DDC 917.204--dc23/eng/20250811

LC record available at https://lccn.loc.gov/2025036699

WWW.SUNSTONEPRESS.COM
SUNSTONE PRESS / POST OFFICE BOX 2321 / SANTA FE, NM 87504-2321 /USA
(505) 988-4418

PROLOGUE

For years my wife, Turza, has pleaded with me to write this chronicle of the misadventures of a 1975 field trip, involving eight Navajos and one *Belagaana* (white person) teacher into Mexico. I knew the stories by heart, but I lacked the continuity and sequence of events as they occurred at the time. While clearing some old storage items from our library closet, I came upon an old metal file box I hadn't addressed in years as far as its use was concerned. There within were old treasures which now needed to be released from captivity and were finally set free to roam in the city dump. But at the very bottom of the file box, I spied a tattered, yellowed envelope. This turned out to be an old letter with railroad embossment addressed to me from my buddy, Warren Roanhorse.

This was the missing link in my reconstruction of a viable story of our journey. I had asked Warren in the summer of 1975 to recreate from memory an itinerary of our trip, day-to-day, through the heartland of the great nation of Mexico. Thanks to Warren's notes, which he sent me later, this is that story. So, hold on to your sombreros and prepare for a hilarious, bumpy ride into a land of mystery and adventure where the only certainty is uncertainty.

CONTENTS

Introduction ~ 9
1. / Prelude to a Journey ~ 13
2. / Proposal for Mexico ~ 17
3. / Expedition Preparation ~ 19
4. / Bon Voyage / Monday, June 16, 1975 ~ 27
5. / Juarez Unbridled / Tuesday, June 17, 1975 ~ 35
6. / Language Classes on Steel Wheels / Tuesday Night, Wednesday and Thursday Morning June 17, 18, 19, 1975 ~ 39
7. / The Sewers of Mexico City / Friday, June 20, 1975 ~ 49
8. / Teotihuacan, Pyramids of the Sun and Moon / Saturday, June 21, 1975 ~ 57
9. / Journey To Oaxaca / Sunday, June 22, 1975 ~ 61
10. / The Great Pacific / Monday, June 23, 1975 ~ 67
11. / Campeche Or Bust / Tuesday, June 24, 1975 ~ 75
12. / Spanish Forts / Wednesday, June 25, 1975 ~ 81
13. / Merida Bound / Thursday, June 26, 1975 ~ 89
14. / Home of the Conquistadors / Friday, June 27, 1975 ~ 93
15. / The Razor's Edge / Saturday, June 28, 1975 ~ 101
16. / Uxmal / Sunday, June 29, 1975 ~ 109
17. / Banditos / Monday, June 30, 1975 ~ 117
18. / Sharks! / Tuesday July 1, 1975 ~ 121
19. / Puebla / Wednesday, July 2, 1975 ~ 125
20. / The Long and Winding Road / Thursday, July 3, 1975 ~ 131
21. / The Calm Before the Storm / Friday, July 4, 1975 ~ 137
22. / El Paso, Gateway to the United States / Saturday, July 5, 1975 ~ 139
23. / The Final Straw / Sunday July 6, 1975 ~ 147
24. / Epilogue, The Circus of Caligula / October 1975 ~155
Author's Note ~ 159
Reader's Guide ~ 161

INTRODUCTION
SPRING 1975

Early spring of 1975 was most promising. Birds were singing, bees were buzzing, and the cats were under the floorboards consummating the season and rather noisily. Everything appeared nauseatingly content and happy now that old man winter finally sobered up and moved on, and good riddance by the way.

The muddy roads would now dry out, and muddy boots could too. Mountain winters were memorable, unfortunately, and not in a good way. Ramah, New Mexico, lies within the congress of the Continental Divide near Osso Ridge (Bear Ridge) along the south side of the Zuni Mountains. All of this in combination constituted the lower "Rockies" of these United States. This mountain range is still a rugged, merciless, incredibly beautiful piece of heaven unknown to most of the world.

As the art teacher at the Ramah Navajo School for the school year 1974 through 1975, the arrival of this desperately awaited season of spring couldn't have come soon enough. The fact that we had lost so many school days due to snow seemed insurmountable, and yet with the sun shining and spring beckoning a positive attitude, anything felt possible. Well, at least on the surface. Let's face it, our end of the school year would have to be extended.

But accepting that though was an altogether other thing. Still, the sun was shining, and the mud was dry. It was time to clear the mind of old winter cobwebs and engage in aspect of a hopeful future.

At that time, the Ramah Navajo School was housed in the old public-school building of the village of Ramah. The school board was leasing the old building while our new school was being built at Pine Hill on reservation land. Ours would be the first Indigenous contracted school without BIA control in the US. There was much riding on our success, and hopefully everyone was aware of it.

The village of Ramah itself, where we were situated at the moment, was a unique quagmire of contradictions. It was essentially a Mormon community, and yet Mexicans, Hispanics, Navajos, Zunis and hippies, who were hiding out from the law or for some other reasons, lived in harmony under a flag of "Live and Let Live." Well, even if that wasn't so, everyone needs a dream.

We few teachers, employed by the Ramah Navajo, in essence, were actually intruders of a sort. We were from all over the continental United States and had never been to this area of the Southwest, much less had an iota of what this place was all about. This new region was far from our own normal fishbowl. Most of us were newly minted educators in the 1970s and lucky to have a job in the first place. Inevitably, none of us had any idea of what an adventure we had volunteered for. This, of course, would be part of our education into a cultural awakening that our host, the Ramah Navajo, would be providing. The only sure thing was, none of us would ever forget the timeless lessons the experience would provide us with for the rest of our lives.

Our students were overall the children of shepherds, weavers, silversmiths, and any employment as far away as Grants and Gallup. If the piñon crop was good in the fall, everyone in the family would stop all their other activities to pick the harvest. The parents would drag the kids out of school to collect this natural bounty of pine nuts from the forest. There was cash in those nuts, that's if you could collect enough of them. It was also a great inconvenience and distraction in the school year's program. When the kids returned, they'd have pockets full of nuts, and if you didn't confiscate them, the classroom floor would look like a chipmunks' convention just exited.

Even so, all things considered, Ramah Navajo kids were a bunch of wonderful challenges. Each was incredibly special in their own sense of themselves. They were good kids, and I felt lucky every day to be part of their lives.

We teachers knew this whole tribal experience was not going to be easy. English here was a new and evolving language and number three after Navajo and Spanish. Expectations and requirements would have to be accompanied, hand in hand, with patience and tolerance. These Navajo children were bright kids being pushed into the 20th century, with many entanglements still in place trying to hold them back to the 19th century. This whole experience was a living, breathing social evolutionary experiment in real time. I wonder if any of us were aware of that. In this situation, we teachers were the students as well.

1
PRELUDE TO A JOURNEY

Christmas of 1974, I rode with Jesse O'Leary on the back of his BMW motorcycle to San Carlos, Mexico. This was my first encounter with Old Mexico and would be one of many a sojourn to this ancient and mysterious land south of our border. Mexico was not just gracious and magical; it was also the *Madre* (mother) of our own state of New Mexico. This introduction to our southern neighbor opened my eyes to the diversity and brilliance of a land culturally superior to our own in its cohesiveness and acceptance of its history and the patience needed to change. I will always be grateful to Jesse for that Christmas morning when he stopped by and asked, "Want To go to Mexico?"

Jesse, himself, was a most unusual character, not that any of us teachers weren't. He sported a motorcycle jacket at all times and shades, from daily classroom to bedtime. He had long dark blonde hair and a small mustache. The only food I ever saw reaching his mouth was Cheetos and his beverage of choice was Pepsi. Jesse was also one of the most well-loved and conscientious math teachers any school was blessed to have. He loved the students, and they him. He understood that patience and repetition were the only sure device of teaching that was going to prove successful in our challenging academic endeavors. Jesse was a damn good teacher, and we were lucky to have him.

That Christmas trip to Mexico, to say the least, made an unforgettable impression on me. It was not the fact that we were lucky to have returned home alive, having survived a vicious blizzard riding a motorcycle at 10° below 0 in 50 miles per hour winds that branded my memory. Nor was it the beauty of the fair weather traveling down through Arizona's Salt River Canyon, with the sunset horizons too astounding to describe, that left me speechless. It was truly Mexico itself, its beauty, humility, and magic. I had traveled most of Europe in 1971 and had seen many of what we consider to be the greatest museums and monuments of mankind. Mexico, though, showed me something I had never experienced before, Mexico showed me its soul.

Mexico knew who she was. Her history and struggle to integrate so many cultures, languages and traditions were a constant contest for her identity. Like a patient, overwrought mother, she would wait until each child found their own way. These were her people, born to her bosom of love and perseverance. They would struggle, and they would somehow survive.

After the impressions that journey bathed me in, I was smitten with an unquenchable thirst to know Mexico better. In the spring of 1975, somehow the absurd idea of a field trip with my male, high school, Navajo students started festering in my brain. What a joke I thought. Who would even consider such an absolutely, ridiculous idea. So, I let the notion rest, knowing there wasn't a chance in hell anyone would take me seriously.

Tom Cummings was a student advisor, grant writer and educational opportunity proposer. As an individual, he was the educational archetype of the early 1960s Great Society. His hero had been JFK, and he followed those great footsteps through to the Peace Corps and later onto the Navajo Reservation. Tom was a gregarious, generous, and yet extremely private person. He was a Catholic, South Boston, Irish boy with the innocent optimism of one who saw so much hope in the 1960s. Now in the 1970s much had changed, but the need to hold onto those "ideals" was more important than ever, and Tom was one of their true ambassadors.

In April, after the thaw began, and spring pretended she might be returning home, Tom had a small party at his trailer at the Cowboy Stopover, a trailer park where many of us teachers and administrators of the new school lived. My roommate, Ron, and I attended along with a few other teachers. As always, somehow Tom had appropriated a couple of cases of Heineken, so we were off to the races. The sun was down, the week had ended, and a bunch of tired young teachers were grateful for the distraction in the middle of our two weeks' pay cycle. The beer and the camaraderie were a welcome balm.

At some point during the evening, Tom sat next to me and inquired what was new at the art department, and I filled him in on the UNM ceramics classes I was teaching for extension college. He feigned interest and redirected the conversation and asked me about my adventure with Jesse to Mexico at Christmas. I took him through the whole descriptive scenario and the resulting life and death contest with the blizzard through which we returned. I finally completed the verbal odyssey with the hope of returning to Mexico again soon. I said I was even toying with the idea of organizing a student field trip to tour Mexico that summer. The idea was, of course, ridiculous. Who would ever consider it the least bit realistic? Tom then stared at me straight in the eyes and said, "Really, why?"

2
PROPOSAL FOR MEXICO

Somehow, Tom had convinced me my Mexican field trip idea was feasible and not ridiculous. With his personal tutoring, I was making a plan for what, as a group, our goals would be for this trip south of the border. The plan was: while traveling, the students would record their daily impressions in a running diary of the journey. They would also photograph and record significant cultural sites. Students would practice Spanish with the Natives. They would learn the currency and clearly calculate the dollar-peso exchange rates. This was an educational opportunity these youngsters couldn't even imagine. Add to that, an unforgettable experience they would carry with them throughout the rest of their lives. In short, it was a dream come true.

What a sales pitch, this could work. If I could bring this project into reality, and the kids returned with photos, manuscripts, and experiences under their belts of world travel, their collective experience would bring personal reflections of life outside this little reservation of the Ramah Navajo. It was a worthwhile endeavor. At least it sounded good.

I typed up my proposal, embellished an itinerary for the summer break in Mexico and proceeded to sell the idea around the campus. Tom had helped me with the concept of the proposal but withheld any of his own personal help in selling it.

"This is your project, Andy, yours alone, be confident and sell it," he said to me.

He was right of course. It was my own screwy idea. In all justification, I believed, no one was going to allow one lone teacher to troop a group of high school Indigenous students into and across a foreign country with no backup other than the utter audacity of a paper plan he schemed up.

So, when this idea of the proposal to Mexico started circulating, I was mystified when I started receiving positive reactions from those in positions of power. What was wrong with these people? Didn't they realize this idea was probably the product of a delusionary mental patient who escaped from some asylum. They actually believed the project had merit, and the students would benefit exponentially from the experience. What the hell, they were buying it. Now I was really in trouble. Seriously, now I was going to have to put up or shut up. Well, no good proposal goes unpunished.

3
EXPEDITION PREPARATION

Yes, the proposal was accepted and applauded. It turns out we had a benefactor supporting the school, who wanted to back just such a project. It didn't hurt to have the endorsement of the school board as well. Somehow, they saw the benefit of enlightening these students to an outside world. Oh no, was this really happening?

Being a member of the literary society didn't hurt in fulfilling this elusive dream either. Our poker club met Wednesday nights and included in the membership was the school director, high school principal, the controller, and other administrative positions. I was the only teacher member and the art teacher at that. When you spent two to three hours a week with a bunch of guys, half Navajos and half old white farts, playing poker, you get close. I'm sure along the way there was help from these compadres of mine. In all probability they were also already placing bets on whether I made it back alive, and if I could bring along my tribal posse as well, huh? Thinking about this, maybe I should have placed a bet also.

The remaining weeks before the summer break were spent planning and preparing. During this time, I met a nice, young, adult education teacher named Warren Roanhorse. Warren, I found out, had six years of high school Spanish. We talked, and he agreed to travel with us as our translator and my assistant. Things were coming together. Since, I myself, had no Spanish other than what little I picked up in Las Vegas, New Mexico, I knew my pigeon slang would not suffice. With Warren, our main travelling language handicap was now remedied. We were going to communicate and integrate with the Native populace just as if we were locals, hot dog.

Next, my roommate, Ron, who was head of the audio-visual department, was going to set us up with two cameras to document our journey. Later he would instruct the students, with the help of Orlando and Cooper Eriacho, his student assistants, on the intricacies of the camera's use. The students would only be using color slide film, in order for us to have a presentation at the school in the fall when we returned. This, above all, was the most important aspect of the adventure, returning with our trip illustrated in film. Proof that we were in Mexico was necessary after all.

The English department put some packets together for writing a traveling diary for each student. They were to keep track, as much as possible, of the events and opportunities during the journey that could be shared with the slide show at the assembly.

A trip to the Mexican Consulate at the old Western Bank Building in downtown Albuquerque was necessary to obtain our traveling visas. At that time passports were not required in Mexico from the US. With that said, I signed in and registered nine new adventurers for a visit to Old Mexico. While there, we also learned we would have to relinquish those visas before we returned to the US. All was very official and documented at the consulate.

The approved money for the trip was to be changed into American Express travelers' checks, $5,000.00 worth. For this transaction, I went to the Merchants Bank in Gallup and signed fifty, one-hundred-dollar checks. It took part of an afternoon. When you counter assigned these checks to the individual merchant of purchase, the check was essentially cash. This at the time was the safe financial vehicle of travel, and it serviced well. We never had a difficulty monetarily speaking.

The students chosen for the trip would need permission letters signed by their parents allowing them this opportunity to travel. I believe many of those parents were relieved just to have the kids occupied with a project for the summer, rather than just lying around looking for trouble. Each student would have to have some sort of small suitcase to hold their clothes and belongings they would need for a six-week trip. That was the proposed schedule at least.

After all the planning and organizing, I felt a need to xerox some pages of conversational Spanish for myself, so I at least didn't appear the teacher dummy who was solely dependent on my assistant translator, Warren Roanhorse. Printing those four sheets of translations would prove the smartest move I made for the trip.

In essence, I believed we were ready. Cameras, film, diaries, visas, suitcases, toothbrushes, traveler's checks and every other contingency had been considered as well. We were as prepared as we were going to be. I thought even the Literary Society had their bets placed, and the percentages and odds well thought-out. We were off to the races.

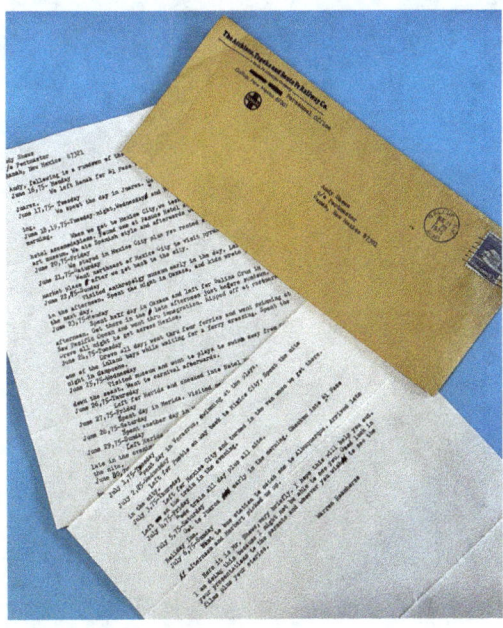

Warren Roanhorse's
1975 Itinerary

Traditional Navajo Hogan

Interior of Hogan

Navajo Sheep Roundup

El Morro National Monument, Ramah, New Mexico

Edgar White,
one of the students on the Mexico Trip

Leon Martine,
one of the students on the Mexico trip

Recording the Elders

Merlin Yazzie and Andy Shows, Publicity Shot
for Gallup Independent Newspaper

4
BON VOYAGE
MONDAY
JUNE 16, 1975

Leaving our old Mormon house rental, I felt exhilarated, terrified, and mystified that this was all actually happening. We were traveling to Old Mexico, seven students, one assistant and me. There were no reservations at hotels. There were no tours or tour guides waiting for us. There was no one and no organization to keep track of our journey. This was "wing and a prayer stuff" that was part of life back then. The only advantage we had, sorry to say, was me. I had been a backpacker in 1971, touring Europe, and was well experienced in day-to-day survival and surprises. But I had only been responsible for one then, and that was myself, not nine. I was obviously going to have to pull my big boy shoes up tight and play the role of all-knowing tour guide.

Would my student's see through my guise of insecurity and realize that I was as uncertain of the future as they were? Well, it was too late to admit it, so pretend, and play the part you have sold to get this trip to Aztlán. You have only yourself to blame.

Herbert Henio was at the school waiting with our van to take us to the border. Herbert was always one of my favorite people. He was an excellent driver, quiet and unassuming. Herbert was solid. He was taking us down the western side of New Mexico and on through to I-25, then straight south to El Paso. Warren Roanhorse appeared right after me. Since I arrived first, we packed our things. With Herbert driving we took off to collect the kids. This would take time since their families were scattered all over the reservation. The great thing was we only had to supply their name, and Herbert would drive us right to their hogan or house or trailer. Still, it did take time.

Later, with the boys collected, we took off on the first leg of our journey south. I stared at our motley crew of students and marveled at the looks of happiness, expectation, and wonder displayed on faces used to only one thing, day-to-day reservation life. They were truly ready for an adventure. During the drive I explained the requirements of the scholastic part of our trip. No one wanted to hear it, but the permission letters to their parents had spelled out how each individual would be required to keep a diary of their experiences while travelling. So, school "was" part of the journey also.

After the mini lecture, which also introduced Warren as our assistant translator, we emphasized the most important rule of travel. We were a pack. We were a collective unit of nine individuals. Our security was essentially dependent on that unity. There could be no strays from the flock; we all were one. Fortunately, I shouldn't have worried so much on this factor. Navajos are a loyal, cohesive group, with a strong natural tribal unity when they are away from the reservation. Individualism expresses itself when they are safely ensconced at home.

As we turned left on Route 36 to Fence Lake, I started examining my traveling family, whom I would be spending six weeks with through an unknown land in search of adventure.

First to consider was Warren Roanhorse. Warren was from the part of the main Navajo Reservation that surrounded the Hopi Reservation. I would come to find out he was also half Hopi. I once asked him if he was all Navajo.

He said, "Yes."

I then asked him if he was Hopi.

He said, "Yes."

I then asked him, "When are you Hopi?"

He said, "When I'm on the Hopi Reservation, of course, I'm Navajo when I'm on the Navajo Reservation."

It all somehow made sense to me. Right?

Chee Dodge Martine, who was sixteen years old at the time, was actually a genius, which meant he was going to be trouble. He was just too bright and bored easily. He would be a challenge, and yet I couldn't not take him, he needed this. I would have to watch him at all times and later occurrences proved this point.

Leon Martine, fifteen years old at this time, was also a handful. Leon was like a hyena in a fun way if you can imagine. He laughed all the time. He stuck by Chee Dodge, they were cousins, and they plotted together in mischief. Still, you couldn't help liking Leon, he was a charmer. He had one of those thousand-watt smiles that made you laugh.

Elvis Natan, fourteen years old, was our smallest and youngest member, and this would pay off when we rented our Volkswagen Microbus in Mexico City. Young Elvis was also quite an artist as a youngster. He illustrated a number of pages of "Tsa Aszi" including a cover once. This magazine was a small enterprising feature the school used to promote the students and life on this small reservation.

Orlando, sixteen years old, and Cooper Eriacho, seventeen years old, were brothers. Cooper was the oldest, but the two were inseparable. Whatever they did, they did together. These two were also "Rockers" and were planning a future together as Native American rock'n'roll idols. They were quiet, thoughtful, and solid. I was glad they were with us.

They also were our photography support group.

Edgar White, sixteen years old, was a surprise member. When I put out the call for travel participants, he showed up one day and said he'd like to go. I don't know if I had ever heard more than ten words out of his mouth before this. Edgar was also a thoughtful, quiet, congenial young man, who had a scar on his cheek I never asked about, and clear unpretentious eyes you could trust. He was a good addition.

Tim Maria was seventeen years old, our oldest student, and he would be a high school senior in the coming year. Tim was an honest, articulate in the Navajo sense, young man who was steady and supportive in a pinch. I would learn to listen to his counsel and as a result, prevent utter catastrophe in a few future events. Tim saved me and our troop with his maturity and patient observance.

This was our party of participants for the great adventure we had prepared. Like it or not, we were ready. Now roll the dice.

Herbert drove us down to Quemado. From there we headed east on Route 60 to Pie Town, down through Datil and onto Magdalena. Finally, we stopped in Socorro, where we had lunch at a Lota Burger. This lunch stop taught me quickly that my students loved hamburgers. To them a hamburger was the bomb. This was an all-important piece of information, for once we crossed the border, food was first.

From Socorro we traveled down the newly paved Interstate 25. In 1975, the western part of the interstate system in the United States was finally being finished. Its completion had been stretched out for years. Finally, after hours and hours, our rickety old school van made it to the outskirts of El Paso, Texas. We were there, this was it, now the real adventure would begin. Herbert dropped us off as close to the border crossing as he could. We waved goodbye to our faithful driver, the last person we knew before we proceeded to the bridge crossing. With our suitcases in hand, we silently said goodbye to the US. We were now totally on our own.

It was late in the day of that mid-June afternoon. Of course, the temperature was unbearable, it was summer in Juarez after all. Our gang of nine marched across the border bridge, and at the entrance to Mexico, we all dropped a dime each into a turnstile to proceed into this foreign land. Culture and poverty shock was immediate, "We're not in Kansas anymore, Dorothy." I had traveled to Juarez before with other teachers, but these students, from some of the poorest circumstances in America, were still taken aback. It wasn't just the poverty and the beggars; it was the filth. I tried to explain to the boys, "Border towns were the worst in Mexico due to so many people being here with plans to just skip across the border sometime soon. None of these individuals were permanent residents, and they could care less about this town. Also, they were not from here and had no plans of becoming local citizens. Even so, if their dreams of the USA did not come to fruition, they might, most unexpectedly, become future Juarez citizenry. Who could say how their luck would run."

Once the first shocking introduction to this rough and ready border situation had finally sunk in, the boys calmed down. We continued in the direction that I had deduced, from a small map I acquired at the consulate, to the train station. It was so damned hot, but we made it there only to find there was no Monday night train to Mexico City. Fortunately, though, Tuesday night there was. This meant we needed rooms for this night in Juarez and new plans for the next day to occupy our time. We needed a hotel. We were all beat and needed a place to rest and regroup.

Searching near the train station, the possibilities were not promising; hell, they were downright depressing. Everything was filthy, and to be totally honest, quite scary. I kept my "Big Boy" mask on and just kept walking, hoping I would stumble into some kind of hostelry where we could plant ourselves.

An old, skinny, derelict, white cowboy witnessed our frustrating search and bird dogged us until he caught up with me. I really wanted to avoid him, but then those magic words left his lips and assaulted my ears, "Need a place to stay?"

Just the smell of this unfortunate soul set our nasal senses on alert, but I responded, "Maybe, why, do you know of a place?"

He grinned, even so, I could tell he needed a drink bad, but he said, "There is a small hotel near the railroad depot, and they could set you up real swell, reasonably priced too."

What choice did I have. I was lost in Babylon. Looking at the gang, I knew they were almost finished, so I said, "Okay, let's have a look." We followed this old, decrepit derelict three blocks and sure enough there was a small hovel of a hotel with a tiny sign stating the obvious, "rooms for rent", and in English. We walked inside to a not so glamorous old movie setting of a western hotel before a gunfight, though there was no bar. There were a couple of ladies sitting on a couch reading magazines, and there was a very dark skinny man at the desk smoking a cigarette.

The old cowboy walked up to the desk and in Spanish explained his new friends' situation, and with a wink that did not escape me, asked if he had three rooms for his new compadres?

I had very little of the language at this point, but I understood *horas* (hours) and comprehended quickly this was a hotel for working girls principally. Even so, the old cowboy and the desk clerk came up with a nightly rate that was impossible to resist. We were too shot anyway; we took it, and the clerk led us to tiny, cubby-hole rooms. The beds and about two feet of extra room was all there was to them, but they would get us through one *noche* (night). After dropping off our bags, we later met at the hotel entrance. The old cowboy was just leaving, slipping out with a handful of pesos. It appeared he'd gotten his commission and was off to another bar to drink the night away, dreaming of the USA, a place he could not return to for some unknown reason only he was privy to. Good luck to him.

We were now in search of food. We strolled down the Avenida 16 de Septiembre, which stated the date of Mexico's independence from the French. Unencumbered of our suitcases, we searched for any familiar sustenance, which hopefully would be hamburgers and French fries, and miraculously we were in luck. A small café/cantina served the food my Navajo boys craved, and I let them eat to their hearts' content. We learned the term *refrescos* (sodas) and asked for Pepsi or Coke. I personally always ordered club soda, though *fria* (cold).

The great thing about border towns back then was that they preferred dollars over pesos, and since that was all we had, there was no currency transaction problem to trouble us. Things were slowly starting to congeal into an unspoken confidential possibility that we were going to be okay. With stomachs full and the sun setting, we made our way back to our hotel. We waved to the ladies working the entrance, found our stable stall-like rooms, and collapsed on our beds with nary a blink of the eye. Our day was done, and we were still alive.

5
JUAREZ UNBRIDLED
TUESDAY
JUNE 17, 1975

The following morning found us a little groggy. It seems our quiet hotel of the daytime was anything but, in the evening. The lobby ladies were quite active and a little noisy to boot throughout the night. We wondered the next day if they were night owls or just preferred the night shift of their occupation. Oh well, we were leaving on the train soon anyway.

The desk clerk allowed us storage of our bags in a small closet behind his office. We took off for breakfast and found *huevos rancheros* (ranch-style eggs) at a little street cafe a few blocks from the train depot. After some good Mexican coffee, we were ready to descend upon the ticket office of the depot and purchase our fares for one-way tickets to Mexico City. Warren Roanhorse read the destination marquee with ticket prices, and together we calculated the cost for nine of us to travel. Money in hand, I marched up to the ticket office, purchased our tickets, second class, and discovered we didn't board until six that evening.

We were marooned in Juarez for the day. There was no other option to the situation. We returned to the hotel.

The desk clerk said, "Not to worry," he'd keep our bags safe. So, we took off to explore the upper and under belly of the city that was Juarez, Mexico.

Taxis were out of the question since there were nine of us, and besides, walking extended our street adventure with day-to-day observances of a major border town. Here, businesses were created out of nothing. A lean-to in an alley could be a car body repair shop. A burned-out storefront could now be an upholsterer's shop, employing teenagers to learn the craft plus protect the premises. There was industry sprouting everywhere and anywhere for these border people willing to just get by. They were obviously survivors.

Our pack wandered through the town and somehow made it to the city *mercado* (market). Since it was summer, we only had to follow our noses to find it. The aroma of fresh fruit and produce led the way into the century-old building. This *mercado* (market) did not sell only food, there were booths with clothing, leather belts, shoes, children's clothing, anything and everything. After all, one had to consider this was 1975, and at the time the word supermarket did not exist in this Mexico. From a vendor we purchased *refrescos* (sodas) and some apples, and after a short break, we decided to continue our local exploration.

I had known about the Zona Pronaf. It was a long walk, but it was the main cultural feature of Juarez. The Mexican Government had financed this project of gathering examples of the country's most exciting arts and crafts to draw the tourists from across the border. It was a noble idea and was well received, but unfortunately it was too far into the future. The Pronaf would not endure a decaying border town's desperation, which was obvious to all that crossed. At the time, the Pronaf was the best draw Juarez had to offer. There was even a glass blower installed there to demonstrate all day long. The restaurants and shops, which surrounded this crafts center, were also the best the city had to offer.

Our gang of nine enjoyed this little adventure. At least I hoped so, and afterward I found a restaurant across from the Pronaf where we were introduced to our first true Mexican cuisine. We ordered burritos for all, which came with beans and rice, of course. It was very different from our New Mexico fare with a choice of green or red chili. Here the food would have a thin sauce of brown or red chili-like sauce. It was nothing near our generous chopped whole green chili inclusion at home. This food informed us, "You are in Mexico now," and this more than anything else, hammered that fact through our thick skulls.

The afternoon was fading, and we realized we needed to start maneuvering back to the train depot. Eventually, we made our way in that scorching afternoon heat to the hotel. We thanked the clerk for our bags. I gave him a dollar, a lot of money back then, and we continued on our way to the station. Just before we entered the depot, I realized we should eat one last time. This trip would comprise two full nights and a day on the train. We had no idea what would be available foodwise to sustain us on this part of the journey. Finding a cafe, the boys packed in hamburgers and *papas fritas* (French fries) and two Pepsis each. They finally appeared ready to go, or at least I hoped they were.

Near six, the train started loading. Seats, open seating, filled in quickly. By the time I got the boys situated in a grouping, there wasn't a seat left in the cab for myself, and I had to move to the next car, oh well. I had given the boys ten dollars each for miscellaneous food and snack purchases while traveling on the train and then proceeded to my seat. Warren had found a seat next to the boys early, so at least he was with them.

It must have taken an hour for the train to thoroughly load with passengers. It turns out that this was the major source of transfer to Mexico City at the time from Juarez. Eventually more buses would replace passenger train transportation, but in 1975 this was still the central mode of that industry. The train itself was a shuffling, shaking, clickety-clacking living museum. All the hardware the cars possessed were remnants of the old Pullmans, and the heavy silver plate of the dining car, which we never used, was straight from the turn of the century. I was certain, Pancho Villa himself had probably used some of these relics.

Just as the train was pulling out, Warren Roanhorse staggered quickly into my train car with a screaming Mexican train conductor behind him. The train was jerking slowly into motion, and I was kind of disoriented by all the commotion. Warren brought the furious conductor into my face. After his exchange with spittle flying in my face, I looked at Warren in panic and said "Warren, what's he saying?"

To which Warren, with six years of Spanish classes, says to me, "I don't know, he talks too fast."

"Oh great," I said.

I followed the conductor to the car, where the boys were seated, and found Leon and Chee Dodge drunk and argumentative. It seems a vendor was selling cheap hooch on the depot landing. Since I had given them ten dollars each, they bought booze and chugged it. I confiscated the remaining liquor and poured it out between the now moving cars, and the conductor appeared placated. That was close. He could have ejected us had the train not started moving. Well, like it or not, we were on our way. Please God, get me through this. Right then I realized, I was going to need help.

6
LANGUAGE CLASSES ON STEEL WHEELS TUESDAY NIGHT, WEDNESDAY AND THURSDAY MORNING JUNE 17, 18 AND 19, 1975

After remonstrating on the near ejection of the group due to Chee and Leon's escapade, I confronted Warren on his Spanish credentials. It turns out, it was my fault, I had never really interrogated him on his specific conversational skills. It appears they were so limited that I, with my pidgin Spanish, obviously, was going to be the major facilitator for communication, great. To make things worse for me, Warren, it turns out, was on salary from the school for the trip, and I wasn't. So now it finally dawned on me, I had one more kid to care for since Warren was no help to me as a translator.

This realization actually hit me like a ton of bricks. I was verbally stranded and totally responsible for eight Navajo individuals in a foreign country. Somehow, we had to survive in this scenario of incomprehensible existence, no language, no currency. This was not good, not good at all. I was in a fix.

Then something whispered in my head, there are four sheets of conversational Spanish in your suitcase. Standing up, careful not to disturb the lady with the baby who shared the seat next to me, I reached up and digging in my small suitcase, found the four pages xeroxed just before leaving Ramah. Thank God, they were still there. Though the sun was setting, I was ready to cram as much Spanish into my limited cranium capacity as possible in the short time available until reaching Mexico City.

So now I had a plan. As darkness fell and my fellow railroad track riding neighbors dozed off one by one, my resolve was set. In the morning, Spanish 101-105 classes would begin in my silly, optimistic, desperation of a situation. Having no alternative is often the only sure success. This resolution established some calm in me, and unknowingly I was drifting off to sleep. Before I faded, I prayed for a miracle, I was going to need it.

Sunrise woke me to babies being fed. It appeared not only did my immediate neighbor have a baby, but the woman across the aisle did also. Trying to follow the conversation of the two, they were certainly friends traveling together with their little ones. Careful not to disturb them, which is impossible for a big, tall blonde oaf, I moved to the next car to check on my crew. Warren had just awakened and appeared no worse for wear. He smiled and said we had passed Chihuahua not long ago. The boys had been sound asleep, so there were no problems. We hoped food would somehow appear magically in the form of burritos or some such. Only time would tell. I moved back to the *madres* (mothers), and being as agile as I could, and tried to seat myself without disrupting the maternal harmony.

The Chihuahuan desert view was distinctively expansive and beautiful. This desert itself, for all intents and purposes, led all the way to Santa Fe, New Mexico, if you ever considered the geography seriously. This desert and the Sonoran were the two natural environmental barriers between our two nations. Only the most rugged of Mexico's citizenry were established in mountain villages and desert pockets, where life somehow stubbornly persisted within this northern territory of the country south of our border.

It suddenly dawned on me; I needed to start gorging myself on the Spanish language. I pulled out the four sheets of conversational text I had xeroxed. It was time to face the music. First, I covered numbers, these were imperative for currency exchange. Secondly, I studied civility, manners, and basic social exchanges that are expected in this particular country. Thirdly, it was how, why, where, when, and who, all supremely dire info clues to any situation. Yet the most important lesson was on one solitary important question, "How much?" The only blessing I had was that before we'd left Ramah, I had discovered these essential lessons and was able to consolidate them into these four sheets of paper. What would I have done otherwise? When you are responsible for eight individuals, you had damn well better be able to communicate somehow to keep them safe. Well, it was time to study, and the clock was ticking. In thirty hours, we would be pulling into Mexico City.

Sitting next to the train car window and reviewing my lessons, I began reciting what I thought were the correct pronunciations of this printed Spanish. Trying to do this quietly was a severe handicap. Still there was no other way. After what seemed like fifteen minutes of this, the mother next to me, I guess finding it impossible to resist, started correcting my pronunciation. Accepting this intrusion with as much grace and gratitude as I could muster, my neighbor indicated she wanted to see the four sheets of language study I was holding.

Upon handing it over, she perused it and shaking her head she informed me, "*Es no Espanol, Mexicano.*" (It isn't Spanish, Mexican.)

Luckily, I caught the gist of her implication, and she reviewed the sheets slowly one at a time. Did I mention that at this point she handed over the baby to me to hold while this was happening?

Probably not, anyway, she covered all four sheets and proceeded to drill me on regional Mexican Spanish as applied correctly to the study sheets.

The baby was a sweet girl, and she just stared at me with my yellow, *gringo* (white person) hair and cooed contentedly. How did I know I was good with babies? Oh well. In the meantime, her mother actually took over as my teacher for a while, and I was slowly starting to get my pronunciation closer to being comprehensible. We would break at train stops along the way, and I would excuse myself to check on my tribe. Later in the afternoon our big stop would be Torreon, but until then there were plenty of smaller stops. Food vendors were more plentiful, so the boys could acquire food and drink. Chee and Leon must have been hungover because there didn't appear to be any new mischief afoot. Hopefully, there would be peace the rest of the way. It helped that the conductor had also been keeping an eye on them, and that greatly contributed to my education progressing.

Somehow there was a pause in my lessons, and the mother seated next to me started speaking to the woman and child across the aisle. There appeared to be an agreement between them of a sort, and they both got up and switched places. I was handed a new baby, a little boy, and my new teacher continued the lessons. It appears the rest I provided them from holding a baby for two days was a fair trade in my continued schooling.

There were no extra seats on this train, so the cost was prohibitive for an extra seat for a child. Still, I was honored to relieve these women of their burdens in exchange for any language skills they could penetrate through my thick skull, and they were making a dent. Trading off was smart because I was now practicing with a different person, and this inadvertently was giving me more confidence in my fluency. The lessons continued, though the girl baby had not been a squirmer like this one was.

These wonderful mothers had brought their own food with them for the trip and even offered to share with this long, gangly *gringo* (white person). I thanked them and politely refused but bought them *refrescos* (sodas) along the way. Realizing the cost of food was dear in Mexico, I would not take food from their mouths but thanked them profusely for the offer. We would take breaks from the lessons and rest, but after twenty or thirty minutes someone would continue the next lesson. It was now at this point I realized the other occupants of our train car were listening. Every so often I heard one interject a correction, and two or three others would add their personal opinions. It turns out, the stupid *gringo* (white person) was becoming an entertaining distraction on this nearly eternal two-day journey by rail. Some people were even laughing along with the mothers as they corrected my pronunciation of something far from the original interpretation. Still the humor and camaraderie of these gracious people warmed my heart as they generously held me in the bosom of the kindness that was Mexico.

Had I not lost my seat in the other train car with the students, I would not have stumbled into this ready learning center of the school of *madres* (mothers). There was no way I could have come close to the almost semi-complete comprehension I was rewarded with thanks to these two good-hearted women. They literally saved our odyssey into Mexico.

We passed San Luis Patos earlier during the night, and as the dawn appeared on my eastern side of the train, it was apparent we were coming to the most northern semi-urban outliers of a city. It must be Mexico City, but it was too soon. We passed Queretaro instead and were now officially on the northern plains leading south to Mexico City. The train started slowing, and I took it we were nearing the station, but I was oh so wrong. At this time, all the old dilapidated and derelict wooden rail cars from before and during the revolution were lined up mile after mile on track after track north of Mexico City. These old rail cars were from the years 1890 to 1910 on average. All that we saw was, in reality, a living train museum. The most fascinating thing though was that they were all occupied. People were living in them. They had become *casas* (homes).

Now I understood the slow crawl of our train's passage. We were moving through these residential homesteaders of a sort, who occupied this northern quadrant of the city, be it ever so humble. Mexico was so poor at the time. I'm sure they just couldn't transform any of this antiquated metropolis and accepted that time and wood rot would do the job for them eventually. Still, witnessing this unbelievable reality in this sad state of the city was a warning signal of the real poverty of this country. Mexico had been through a lot and was seemingly holding on by its fingernails.

I kissed the babies, hugged the *madres* (mothers) and thanked them profusely for saving our student field trip in the few words they had taught me. After a long goodbye, with other passengers also wishing me good fortune and *via con Dios* (go with God), I moved to the boys' car and checked in with Warren. The whole gang was now excited and eager to leave this rail berth from Hell. Two days on a train was something a Navajo never experienced nor had known anyone else who had. I'm sure their grievances would be well known when they returned home.

Warren and I started organizing the boys and preparing them for the eventual departure. The train continued its sluggish crawl south. It just went on and on. Was it ever going to end? Soon we started seeing the end of the revolution-era train cars, and the normal railroad construction of workshops and warehouses started to appear. We were finally arriving at the depot of Mexico City. The enormity of that fact didn't escape us. There appeared out of nowhere a large, old, white Cadillac ambulance with the customary red crosses on it, parked next to the tracks. As we approached the depot, there was an obvious off-duty nurse straightening out her white uniform while smoking a cigarette. She was leaning on the vehicle while another nurse, legs splayed, with some guest between them, completed the commerce of the moment. This is what my crew and I witnessed first-hand from the train car windows as we pulled into and stopped at the depot, "Welcome to Mexico!"

The old train station of Mexico City, Estasion La Villa, was our disembarkment location. This was an old and grand dame of a French and Spanish-styled complex and had seen better days, and yet it was still standing. Warren and I gathered the boys and made our way to the depot's entrance. There, it was a certainty, would be no shortage of taxis. All the drivers knew the train schedule and were there for lucrative fairs from exhausted, short tempered train warriors, who just wanted to get to their final destination. Standing on the curb I was assaulted by a taxi pimp, who waved over a couple of cabs for us. We would need two for the nine of us. I asked the lead driver for a decent municipal hotel, not too expensive since we needed three rooms. He suggested the Hotel Panucho, and it was located in the historic district. It sounded good, so I informed the other taxi driver of our destination, and we took off.

Memories of the train were fading as the taxis fought the downtown traffic of the city. We eventually arrived at our hotel. The Hotel Panucho was a four-story affair from the turn of the century and was appealing in a nostalgic sort of way. It felt safe also. Paying the taxis off, I became aware I would need pesos *pronto* (soon). The drivers and I worked out the exchange in dollars, but it was an imposition. At the border, dollars were actually the preference, but deep in country, it was obvious this was their country thus their currency. Wake up, Andy.

We purchased three *cuartos* (rooms) for the nine of us and settled in. Just to stretch out flat on a bed after the last forty-eight hours was ecstasy. With young boys, of course, after about half an hour, they were ready to go again. I had appropriated a Mexico City map from the consulate in Albuquerque.

Discovering the *Palacio De Bellas Artes* (Palace of Fine Arts) was nearby, I decided our first cultural sojourn should be to there. When we arrived at its location, we were in awe of its beauty. The building itself was a beautiful structure of French design, a little piece of Paris. The exhibition within was a more recent historical review of Mexican artists important to any new arrival visiting this country. Orozco, Rivera, and other muralists plus many others of varying art forms did not disappoint. The rich colors and organic shapes, the emotive messaging of the artists communicating their country's struggles, all of this was frequently beyond words. Even so, I had eight young Navajos who had never been to a foreign country much less out of New Mexico. We walked through the galleries and halls, and I tried my best to explain what all of this meant. The art, the imagery, let's be honest, they were just kids, and most could care less. Still, it was an introduction to another people's lives whether they liked it or not. The result was that nothing was lost on them completely. They took pictures, shared cameras, and things felt positive.

After the *Palacio* (Palace), we walked to the adjacent park of Alameda Central. Here there were organ grinders with monkeys. The boys loved that along with all the beautiful young *senoritas* (young women) who were in attendance in the park. There were also jugglers and proselytizers pushing some form of Jesus. Life was an infectious possibility in this city, it had to be, this was the last chance for many here. Mexico City, the *madre* (mother) of its people, had to somehow keep them all fed and alive as well.

One of the key acts of nutritional assurety for this country was an official act, thanks to the revolution, to officially lock down the price of tortillas and beans. These two commodities sustain the population through the most doubtful of times. The bean burrito served as breakfast, lunch, or dinner. The beans could be refried, boiled, and even made into soup. It was a simple fact that pinto beans drove this labor force's engine.

There tended to be an unavoidable frequency of sidewalk bypasses, due to the huge mounds of dirt at inconvenient locations along the way. Closing in on one of these inconvenient heaps, we discovered a sign stating the Mexican subway system was being excavated on this route, and these gravel obstructions turned out to be more prevalent the more we toured the city. Later, while walking the Avenue Paseo de la Reforma, we would see large plexiglass cubes covering magnificent Toltec and Aztec artifacts recovered from the subway excavations. But they were just sitting there with no one guarding them—there was just so much recovered. It was obvious, even the pedestrians had lost interest. I was personally in shock. Here were millions of dollars' worth of history for the taking, and no one showed the least interest. Later I would discover that Mexico City sat on thousands of years of one of the most spectacular archaeological treasure chests in the world. Now, of course, covering it was a sprawling modern city where once there had been floating gardens and vast, rich, ancient cities. Still the fascinating fact of this boundless history was breathtaking to say the least.

My tribe was losing interest. It felt time for a real regional meal in traditional style, and everyone was hungry. We were lucky and found a small family *cocina* (kitchen). The place had five tables total. We took up the extra-large round table in the back of the room. This was family-style dining. There were seven courses starting with a bean soup, of course. The food kept coming, and the boys, after two days on a train, did not object to any of the traditional fare. The meal was sumptuous and delicious and ended, most certainly, with the traditional flan. These little family-style restaurants were simply the best. I wonder if you could even find one anymore with fast food infecting the whole world's palette. The price for all the splendid service and a most delicious meal was impossibly *barato* (cheap). I hate that word, but fiscally I don't know how these people kept the doors open. Somehow this was just another reminder of how dire every single peso was to Mexicanos at the time.

With our stomachs full and the hour not quite late enough to return to the hotel, I saw a marquee to a *cine* (movie theatre). Unbelievably, there was a Kung Fu movie showing which was the perfect venue for young high school aficionados. The tickets were equivalent to twenty-five cents each. I need to mention, at our hotel I had signed over a traveler's check for a handful of pesos which inevitably got us nicely through for the rest of the day. The Kung Fu movie turned out to be Korean with Japanese subtitles, which were then followed by Spanish subtitles, which the boys had me then try to translate into English. With some of the forty words of Navajo, Sam Alonzo, who taught Navajo at our school after hours, had taught me. By the end of the movie my brain was a slurry of gibberish, but the gang appeared to have been thoroughly entertained despite it all. They'd had fun and combined with train fatigue; they were finally beyond ready to hit the sack. Warren and I got them back to the hotel and applauded ourselves for getting them through another day alive and out of jail.

7
THE SEWERS OF MEXICO CITY
FRIDAY
JUNE 20, 1975

Sleep was good that night, though I felt a little gurgling in my lower intestine. After the last two days, I chalked it up to nerves. We had finally agreed on roommates to each room. Poor Edgar White would have to somehow survive Chee Dodge and his cousin, Leon. I would say a prayer for him. The next room I knew would be no problem the Eriacho brothers, Cooper and Orlando, would share with little Elvis Natan. Tim Maria would share the last room with myself and Warren. This served Warren and I well since Tim was far more mature, and we could share plans with him. He probably had a better head on his shoulders than the two of us. Tim would become invaluable.

The morning of the 20th we met in the hotel lobby, and then we moseyed on down the street to get breakfast. At breakfast I informed the boys they would start their journals that morning, and Warren, Chee Dodge, and I would proceed to the Banco National to cash travelers' checks. From there we would continue on to a car rental agency, of which we had seen a few, and attempt to rent something accommodating the nine of us on an extended journey. In case you hadn't noticed, I mentioned taking Chee Dodge with us. You just don't miss anything---better the devil with you than left at home.

We three wandered down Balderas Boulevard in search of the bank we needed. It was a lovely, unusually clear day. The traffic had finally slowed down. Everyone was now at work. The bank should be opening momentarily as we strolled towards it, and that was all I remembered.

As my consciousness slowly started returning, I realized I was being restrained. Somehow, I was incapable of moving my limbs. There were scuffed shoes passing by my eyes. Where was I? Slowly I looked up and saw Warren and Chee Dodge in an incredibly, intensive battle of the Navajo language. This was a major conflicting debate, and as I started to come to, it dawned on me that they were discussing my fate.

My chin and elbow were all, it turns out, that were keeping me from dropping the remainder of the way into the main sewer thoroughfare of Mexico City. Obviously, city maintenance had pulled this sewer cover plate, and either had forgotten it or were returning to do some work later. In observing the beauty of the city, like the fool, I had stepped into the entrance of doody Hell itself, a manhole, wide open and awaiting a victim. I was now stranded, dangling in this precipice to the underworld. Thank God, I had my crew with me to haul me out, right? They were going to pull me out, right? Why were they taking so long to help me?

As my chin and elbow were tiring, I felt I might slip away or be nibbled away from the bottom up by the *ratas* (rats). My "buddies" finally reached down and dragged me out of Hell's invitation. In all that time, no Mexicanos ever interfered. Maybe the *gringo* (white person) owed those two-cowboy hatted *Indios* (Indians) money, who knew. I saw a lot of shoes go by, and everyone minded their own business.

Finally standing up, my "buddies" helped straighten me out, so I could walk again. We proceeded to the bank. Fortunately, the sewer hole was drier at the top, and its residual "Ode de natural" wasn't too intrusive. The bank didn't seem to mind. I cashed a large number of checks into pesos. We would need them once we left the city and moved into the rural countryside. When traveling in a foreign land it is best not to assume there will be banks or *cambios* (money exchanges) in places tourists tended not to travel. The truth is, in places without money, why would you need banks anyway.

Flush with pesos, the three of us, thanks to the directions from the bank, hiked to a promising car rental agency. We were in luck. The delightful young lady at the desk spoke English and had a Volkswagen Microbus that would serve our needs splendidly. We'd hit the jackpot, ha! This wonderful young woman compiled all the detailed paperwork, including insurance. She copied our visas, which I had, then sat down with me and worked out a route through Mexico that would allow us the maximum experience on the safest and most suitable highway routes. She and I marked this promising passage on a map the agency supplied us with, and I now felt I had accomplished the main travel goal needed for a safe trip—money, vehicle, and mapped excursion. We could now go forward.

We left the rental car agency and made it back to the hotel. The gang had been getting antsy, and Tim said we were not a minute too soon. Warren and I loaded up the crew, after figuring out seating, and made a straight shot for Chapultepec Park on Paseo de la Reforma. It turned out the key to the configurative seating was Elvis Natan. You see, the seating was three to a row, but the front was centered with the stick shift. There were few VW automatics in 1975. But we were fortunate, there was only one student small enough to fit in this middle seat and most likely survive to have children one day---that would be Elvis, God bless him. Warren and I took especially good care of Elvis. He was also a great kid.

We made it to the park and miraculously found parking. It was a Friday, so our timing had been good. Marking the location of the van in our minds, we strolled the park and ran right into, of all things, a hot dog vendor. The dogs were odd, we'd never know what breed they were, but they were sure tasty and hit the spot. With *refrescos* (sodas) and chips, we were finally ready for this city park adventure. The park in 1975 was pretty bare. There were some scraggly trees and bushes, but nothing like the beautiful park that exists today. There were vendors of all sorts selling everything, whether they were strolling or standing at a booth. It was a certainty that no one was licensed for any of this, but who was going to stop it. Hell, probably half the cops in the city had relatives selling their wares here.

We hiked up the drive to the Chapultepec Palace, where the French had established ownership of Mexico for five dismal years. Before that, this palace was the residency of the president of Mexico, Benito Juarez, and before that at some time, the Viceroy of Spain. The American flag had even been raised here also to end the Mexican American War. I personally consider the events leading up to and following this historic episode, our greatest embarrassment as a nation for the United States of America. Shame on us.

The students were enjoying all this impetus, and stretching our legs was, also, just about what the doctor ordered. The palace was extensive and impressive, but it was the views from the palisades that took our breath away. The entire city was at our feet. Later we hiked much of the park. We visited some small museums of murals and other things and finally discovered the way to the great Anthropological Museum of Mexico. Time was up though; we would have to plan this another day. The sun was reminding us of the time, and my young soldiers had fulfilled their duty this day. It was time to return them to their barracks. We rediscovered the van, loaded up, and I drove us through early evening traffic to our Hotel Panucho. Once parked, we would fill up on *hamburguesas* (hamburgers) and *papas fritas* (French fries) and drink *refrescos* (sodas) at the tiny, outdoor café. Then we would drag ourselves to our beds, and that is exactly what we did.

Just before sleeping, I asked Warren about the sewer incident. He didn't say anything. Maybe he didn't hear me. I repeated myself.

Warren then said, "Chee Dodge wanted to leave you to the sewer. He said we could have so much more fun without you." I argued with him, but he was obstinate about leaving your white ass behind!

Hearing this I asked, "What changed his mind?"

Warren looked me straight in the eye with a big smile on his face and said, "Well, I explained to him finally, that only you had all the money and checks, and he wouldn't get very far without them."

This revelation stunned me and yet after consideration, what did I expect. This was Chee Dodge Martin. That night I had a lot to think about to say the least. Eventually, I started fading, but that gurgling in my intestine appeared to be increasing, nerves? The last thing I remember that night was ridiculous. Was that a rattle being shaken ever so lightly near me, huh? Don't be silly.

Palacio de Belles Artes, Mexico City

Teotihuacan Mexico City

Plaza of Teotihuacan Mexico City

Olmec Head, Museum of Anthropology

Tienda in Mercado Selling Religious Items

Crafts Market Mexico City

Organ Grinder Without Live Monkey

8
TEOTIHUACAN, PYRAMIDS OF THE SUN AND MOON SATURDAY JUNE 21, 1975

Saturday morning found me occupying our *bano* (bathroom). Something was wrong, needless to say, there was a great cleansing occurring in my body. Eventually, I reappeared to the world a new person and proceeded to organize the crew for breakfast at the cafe and plans for the day. We were going to travel northeast of the city and drive straight up to Teotihuacan, one of the greatest pyramid and temple complexes in greater Mexico. The boys had no concept of what this journey would reveal to them as far as the monumental impact of these incredible ancient ruins. To them the Anasazi were ancient, and their rock and adobe structures were prevalent on the reservation. For me this would be the beginning of collecting their first impressions of the vastness and might of an awe-inspiring empire, whose tentacles of trade reached all the way into New Mexico.

The drive out of the city wasn't bad. It was Saturday, and the traffic leaving the city wasn't weekday rush hour. Soon we connected with

Route 85, which took us a distance to the Teotihuacan ruins. At this time the whole area was just dirt, but not far from the site farmland bloomed. There were *maize* (corn) fields everywhere and in the middle was the magnificent mega wonderland that was the complex of the sun and moon pyramids. It was just so, so vast.

We had to stay together, even with the complex stripped free of vegetation, it was just too far beyond vast. There were no crowds. There were a few stray tourists, climbing the structures and photographing. The boys had their cameras out, freshly loaded with slide film, and started shooting. The only problem was, there was so much to record on film. We stayed together and started climbing the pyramid of the moon. There were no restrictions on ascending the pyramids back then as there are now. We essentially had carte blanche to climb everything, and we did. The views, my God, the views were incredible. Was this why they were built—for the Aztec to marvel at the eminent greatness of their empire? The plazas, ballparks, marketplaces, not to mention the palaces and temples, were beautiful in structure today, just to imagine them in their past glory was beyond comprehension. We hiked the entire complex, and that is saying a lot.

On completion of our adventure, we found a taco vendor near the parking lot. We ordered lunch *con refrescos* (with sodas) and sat near the van. Suddenly, a red emergency light went on in my head, and I excused myself to some rows of corn bordering the parking lot. Any bathrooms were further within the ruin's complex and too far to make it in my now delicate condition. Our incredible excursion complete, we loaded up the van for our return journey. It had been a great day, even Leon and Chee were smiling.

Late in the day, we finally arrived back at the hotel. The city was celebrating Saturday off from work, so what the hell, we needed to experience some other stimuli. I found an arts and crafts market on the map (still located there today), and our whole tribe hiked up avenues east of our hotel and discovered it. The whole complex was a fiesta of color and form. There were pinatas, maracas, leather belts, dresses, sombreros, guitars, heck, everything. It was visually too much to even fathom. We stayed together, which was the hardest part. Soon, I gave up and told everyone to meet up at the entrance in half an hour. There was no booze around, so that wouldn't be a problem. Each boy was given the equivalent of fifteen dollars in pesos to make a purchase of something they liked. This would force them into some form of social intercourse, like it or not.

Without intention, I discovered a leather side pack with strap that I could keep all the receipts I had collected, and the notebooks, which recorded non-receipt transactions such as taco vendors. The pack was large enough to hold the boys' diaries and slide film also. This purchase would be indispensable in our travels or so I thought.

In forty minutes, the boys started showing up. I had been frantic up to this point, but then I remembered that only Warren and I possessed a watch. Warren had purchased a new straw cowboy hat, which he beamed proudly under. Three of the other boys purchased new hats also. Cooper and Orlando, our Indian rockers, purchased beautiful Mexican guitars. It was amazing what fifteen dollars could buy in Mexico back then. Finally, collecting everyone after appreciating their purchases, we searched for a cafe. It was dark now. It had been a good day.

Not far from our hotel, we found a café/cantina willing to make us *hamburguesas* (hamburgers) and *papas fritas* (French fries). I drank *aqua mineral con gas* (sparkling mineral water), thinking this would help relieve my gastral situation. The meal was surprisingly good considering, and we made it back to the hotel not too late. Everyone was sun exhausted from the day of hiking the pyramids. Students were also happy, maybe even joyful, with their purchases and the awareness that they could communicate in another country. This was an accomplishment they could be proud of.

We bedded down in the pleasant exhaustion of new explorers. I was certain there would be dreams of adventures to come amongst the kids, they'd done great. As for me, my roommates snored away as I sat at the throne of misery, dedicated to what I would come to know as Moctezuma's Revenge. I had not been aware, but I finally accepted this penance was due me for my white skin. Eventually I made it to the bed and lay my head down. The struggle to sleep was finally won, and again as I drifted off, I most definitely heard a rattle and a hum.

9
JOURNEY TO OAXACA
SUNDAY
JUNE 22, 1975

Sunday morning was quiet. At breakfast I informed the group on our day's agenda and the ultimate travel goal of our trip. We were going as far, if not further, to Merida. This was the capital of the Yucatan and the heart of Mexican Maya country. This was essentially the center of Maya civilization, ancient and contemporary. We would learn much there.

There was one stop first we had to make before leaving the city, the fabulous Anthropological Museum of Mexico. Fortunately, the museum opened early, and we could begin our cross-country odyssey from there.

After closing our account at the hotel, we packed the back of the minivan with all our belongings plus guitars. Miraculously, we had just enough room to pull this off. Having concluded our business at the hotel and thanking the staff, we revved up our engine and pulled into Sunday traffic and easily snaked our way back down Paseo de la Reforma. We parked outside the Museum of Anthropology, and the whole crew bailed out of the van and entered the hallowed halls of this great bastion of Mexico's ancient history.

Fifty years later, I would recognize a stone carved sculpture of a rattlesnake I had originally observed on a pile of excavated dirt from the subway. It had been protected solely by a plexiglass cube along with many others, but now it was on display in one of the most impressive modern presentations I had seen anywhere in the world. I doubt anyone will ever know how much of the museum's present collection came from under the streets of Mexico City in that 1970s subway excavation.

Even at that time in 1975, the museum was handsomely appointed with the Olmec heads from north of Veracruz and the fabulous Toltec turquoise jewelry, which possessed stones traded as far as away as Chaco Canyon and exchanged for Macaw feathers and copper bells. The fabulous Mayan exhibits were the teaser for our future exploits into the Yucatan. It was all so much, but at this point, it was still new to the students, and they impatiently permitted me to explain it to them.

In a couple of hours, it was apparent a road trip was calling our names. The Sirens of the road demanded our attendance, so we departed the bastion of ancient history, loaded up, and joined the traffic flowing south towards Oaxaca. We eventually connected with Route 164 south of the city. Later, at Izucar de Matamoros we flowed into Route 190, the Panamanian Highway. We were driving through mythical country. The views were often inexplicable. Mountain ridges still colored in the remaining mid-morning light were guarding small villages with steepled churches, hidden in plain sight. The landscapes, farms, and pasture lands were a panorama of beauty. Truly, there were no words to justify description. We were mesmerized by our observances. I knew the boys were impressed because there wasn't a peep out of them. We passed through Acatlan de Osorio and Tamaztilapam farther down the road, and inevitably we reached the outskirts of Oaxaca just after the little village of Etla.

This had been one hell of a trek, but the drive showed us the kilometers we could cover if necessary. Being Sunday had helped considerably. Oaxaca was no Mexico City. It was more a large sprawling Santa Fe with a double *zocalo/plaza* (square) and charming hacienda-style architecture, appearing everywhere and displaying a relaxed comfortable atmosphere over the city. I believe we were immediately smitten by Oaxaca; the Sirens had been right to call us here.

It was now late afternoon, and we needed rooms for the night. With luck, we discovered a charming old hotel with an open inner courtyard to all the rooms. We found three *cuartos* (rooms) on the second floor with balconies overlooking the courtyard with breakfast seating for the next morning. *Fortuna* (fortune) was with us. We grabbed our bags and got ourselves installed into our new digs. After a few minutes respite including my intestinal preoccupation, we met in the lobby, and I and my crew of straw-cowboy-hatted Navajos continued our "Grand Tour" of the city of Oaxaca. Although the hour was now late, our excitement at this new city, which was so different from the urban sprawl of Mexico City, just intensified as we walked amongst Sunday strollers on the sidewalks of local streets surrounding the *zocalos* (squares). This was another Mexico we were being introduced to, a Mexico of peace and harmony and prosperity. This was the Mexico of Benito Juarez, in my opinion, the greatest leader this country ever produced. So much so did I believe this, that my one and only son's middle name is Benito, in homage to this great man.

A wonderful street cafe called to us when our fuel tanks were reaching empty, and we presented ourselves to a cornucopia of regional cooking never before possible until now. Some of the boys still ordered *hamburguesas* (hamburgers) and *papas fritas* (potatoes), but Tim Maria tried the green corn tamales covered in a regional sauce with beans and rice. Warren and I tried something called chicken mole. I have been addicted to this dish still after fifty years. The meals were sumptuous and generous in portions, and our obvious pleasure and gratitude were apparent to the cafe manager and waiters.

The walk back to the hotel was peaceful, and the night clerk welcomed us with eyes wide open upon seeing eight Navajos and one tall *gringo* (white person). I imagine him thinking, "What ta hell is this about?" Oh well, it will give him something to keep him awake tonight. We hit the sack except for me. The urgency of the *bano* (bathroom) was demanding my attendance, *pronto* (soon). I made it just in time. Vesuvius erupted. Finally, back in bed, I was becoming aware that the Teutonic shifts in the faulty foundation of my intestinal being was not going to be resolved, and I would have this unpleasant reality to contend with for the duration of the trip. Drifting off finally, I distinctly heard a voice speak in a choppy, Indio tongue that I was, of course, not familiar with, and a rattle again being shaken most abruptly, insistently. "What the heck?"

Madonna Altar in Oaxaca Mercado

Juarez Mural in Oaxaca

Cathedral on Oaxaca's Zocalo

10
THE GREAT PACIFIC
MONDAY
JUNE 23, 1975

The next morning found us at breakfast in our hotel's beautiful courtyard. Birds were flying over us in the trees within these confines. The sunlight was glorious in this early Eden-like setting. Let's face it, this was heaven. Breakfast itself was a piece of bliss—simple and delicious. Of course, Mexican coffee, as always, was beyond compare. Why couldn't this exist in the US?

After the dishes were cleared away, I passed out the diaries, and through the moans and groans, the boys started recording the last two days' events. Much had been seen, and much would need retelling. Their versions of this adventure would be individual accounts to add to the group's general record.

In time, we collected ourselves for a tour of the city proper. The map the car rental agency had given us, was actually superb and led us to the cathedral and other high points of Spanish Colonial architecture. This was not only a beautiful city, but it was also a gracious respite to all who journeyed here from afar. In the *zocalos* (squares) there were street performers of every sort, and they were from all over the world. We saw jugglers, mimes, magicians, even brief staged acts of Shakespeare in Spanish. I was gob-smacked by this unprecedented production of world culture as varied as the visitors themselves. Benito would have been proud that his home city swelled with such hope and promise for the human condition.

Oaxaca was the Mexico the world needed. Near noon, it was decided we were ready to depart. We checked out of our little piece of heaven and packed the van. Our plan was to make it to Salina Cruz to observe the Pacific Ocean. With no traffic to contend with in the early afternoon, we glided out easily from Oaxaca's city center and continued down Route 190. The drive was most pleasant. In addition, I now started carrying a wad of toilet paper in my jeans for emergencies, so my stress level was lowered.

As we were driving southeast, we became aware this part of Mexico was incredibly vast with farmland and gentle mountain ridges mixing up the vista. There was another unique aspect to our trip that caught our attention, which we never expected. Mexico was a mobile car museum. In 1975 in our VW Microbus, we were driving amongst Ford Model Ts and As. There were Studebakers and Studs Bear Cabs. It appeared all the old "Dust Bowl" pickup trucks made it down here also. It was simply amazing. One of the marvels of invention and ingenuity that kept these objects of living history running was, of course, bailing wire. I saw old axles wrapped with pounds and pounds of it. God bless the innovation of survivors. They will certainly inherit the earth.

The further southeast we drove, the fewer cars we passed. We bypassed villages like San Pedro Totolapan and San Juan Lajarca and observed village sizes appearing to contract. My guess is this land would not support the agriculture needed for any significant populations. One must keep in mind this was the year 1975, and these were hard times, not just for Mexico, but for much of the world. When we got somewhere near Magdalena, the smooth sailing we had been experiencing abruptly came to an end. The earth appeared to drop off a cliff, and we were now descending on a series of switchbacks. I kid you not, it took two hours before we arrived at level earth again. The smell of burning brakes was the only heavy scent in the van that entire time. This ordeal had felt never-ending. We had no idea of what we had gotten ourselves into. It turns out that we were descending the upper plateau of Mexico proper and dropping into the beginning of the tropical foothills, which would guide us into the eventual Yucatan.

When we reached the bottom of our descent, we were able to make a straight shot down Route 185 to Salina Cruz and the Pacific Ocean. We stopped at the coast, and the boys were able to play in the vast, cold, green Pacific waters. They were impressed; these were desert kids. To them, Ramah Lake was as close to an ocean as many of them would ever see. This would also be their first taste of salt water.

Suddenly, as we were driving away from the beach, it dawned on me that there was no town of Salina Cruz. I had hoped we would bunk down in some pension or hostel or such, but no go. With the sun going down, we decided to follow 185 back and continue on it since it was the main artery to cross the Isthmus of Mexico to the Gulf of Mexico. Following this route, our motley crew would see that body of water probably early tomorrow. Unless we found lodging, that became our plan. But firstly, we needed food and bathrooms.

As we were leaving Salina Cruz, a couple of miles up the road, there was a very small office shack adobe building, standing in the middle of nowhere. Nearing it, an old man came out and started waving us down. I had no intention of stopping for this unknown person, but Warren, who was concentrating on a sign on the building, advised me to halt and I did. This was the problem with poor countries with no money. Their officials often had no uniforms or insignia to identify their position. Thus, you could often find yourself in a hotbed of trouble, even litigation, for not recognizing them. Warren saved us a heap of trouble. We stopped, our visas were requested, and the old gentleman went into his small singular office and stamped each one. In no time, we were on our way and none the worse for wear.

We drove to Juchitan. There wasn't much there, though we did find a restaurant. The parking lot was empty, that should have given us some warning, but hunger beats expectation every time, so we stopped and went inside. This so-called restaurant was big and spartan. No one met us at the entry, so we just seated ourselves. I gather our noisy disruption awoke someone from the back, and we were eventually attended by a skinny meek little man who eyed us with great suspicion. Something should have warned me there was a problem, but the kids were hungry. I asked for menus, and this individual retrieved some and passed them around. By this time, I had enough comprehension to translate some of the regional fare. The waiter, who knows what position he actually was, disappeared and didn't return for an eternity. Now the boys were getting more restless by the second. After half an hour, the person attending us returned and took our order hesitantly. What was going on? We waited. After another half an hour, Warren and I decided to invade the kitchen and see how our meals were coming along. At this point, we noticed there weren't even any cooking smells from the kitchen. We entered through the swinging kitchen doors to an empty kitchen, not of two employees or pots and pans or stoves and sinks, but of food. Nowhere was there a potato, a bean, or even a tortilla. This restaurant was empty of saleable, consumable products. We confronted the two men in the kitchen, who were frightened of our aspect, and they revealed they were trying to get groceries and didn't know when that would be.

Warren and I were furious. We told the kids. With all of us starving, and screaming, and shouting, we marched out of there with empty stomachs. Continuing up the road, we knew we would hit some other village, right? It was then that I noticed our vehicle's gas tank gage was on half, and I had not seen a Pemex station in a long, long time. Matias Romero was the only major town on this entire stretch of 185. We would fill up and eat there, right?

It was dark now; the boys were fading from hunger into sleep. The air was tepid, and all the windows were opened for air. We were entering the jungle through the Isthmus of Mexico. In no time at all our windshield was covered with locusts, beetles, moths, bats, and creatures we would never understand had a right to even exist. This was a world we were not prepared for. The bugs were flying in the windows as we drove, and there was nothing we could really do about it with the claustrophobic heat of the jungle.

We reached Matias Romero about ten o'clock. The town was closed up tight, and thus there was no food, no gas. We would have to continue on. There was no other alternative. I looked at the map now that petrol was the priority. No gas, stuck in a suffocating endless jungle, and the alternatives of being eaten alive should we run out of gas was not a favorable impression. If we could make it to Jesus Carranza, they would certainly have petrol of some kind, even if we had to wait till morning for them to open up?

There was one other possibility, if we chanced it, and that was a place called Guichicovi. This was off the main road five miles; but might we risk it, we did. By now it was eleven-thirty. We drove to what was a tiny village along a road off 185 W and eventually found a town all lit up. We drove through it and discovered the lights were from store display windows, where coffins of all sorts and sizes and qualities were presented for glorious display, window after window after window. This town obviously only produced coffins and nothing else. Shucks, this didn't bode well. We were already on edge expecting to be eaten by the jungle as it was. We skedaddled out of there and returned to Route 185 north.

I, personally, was running out of gas, so I asked Warren to drive. Now 185 was a rough, beat up, potholed highway you wouldn't wish on your worst enemy, but that was our route, like it or not. When the road suddenly smoothed out in my sleep, I woke myself after a while and observed a shiny, newly blacktopped, smooth drive of a road. Hell, this was wonderful, I said to Warren, "Heck, Warren, this is great!"

To which he responded, "Yeah, I saw this fork to a better road, and I took it."

Finally awakened enough, I said, "We're not on that highway anymore?"

And unbelievably he said, "No!"

After my panicked, chastisement eruption was over and I hadn't killed him, I informed Warren even though this was a nicer road, it would probably lead us into some pot grower's estate, and we would all be either eliminated or enslaved.

"Oh," says he.

Our tank was now on empty. We were going to live out the rest of our lives competing for food with iguanas in the jungle. I turned around and kept driving. We reached 185 again and headed north. The only consolation was the familiar rattle and bang from the potholes on this highway to Hell, but we knew we were at least going in the right direction. I don't know how, the angels must have been watching over us, but we made it to San Martin. Again, another small village locked up tighter than, well you know. How were we still running? The fuel needle had nowhere else to go. The end was certainly near, sorry guys.

It was two-thirty in the middle of the jungle in the Isthmus of Mexico, dividing the Yucatan from the main corridor of the Mexican Highlands. We were out of luck, or were we? Up ahead, Elvis Natan suddenly piped up and said he saw a green light through the trees. The Pemex signs were green. This was too much to ask for after our run of bad luck. But sure enough, there it was, all by itself in the middle of the jungle like a beacon to a fuel oasis. We drove straight to it and ran out of gas fifty feet from the pumps. Exhausted, they stumbled tired and hungry out of the van and pushed the behemoth VW to the pump with Elvis's steering. We had made it.

There were two attendants who were awake and wide eyed, staring at eight Indios in cowboy hats and one tall lanky *gringo* (white person). *Que paso* (what's happening)? We got the bus to the pump and ordered Nova not Extra (expensive gas) and started to relax. The boys relieved themselves on the side of the road in the bushes. I hurriedly asked for the *bano* (bathroom) and was directed to a door at the side of the station.

I will not describe this welcome station of intestinal relief. Suffice it to say, any interior shot in the film "Midnight Express" of the Turkish prison, was a vast improvement to this space. There was not a seat of repose to this porcelain throne. Paper for swabbing the remains of the day was nonexistent. Thank God, I had my pocket full of tissue. The release of residual bodily afterthought, jettisoned at the speed of a sonic boom. I was surprised the porcelain withheld the impact. Mexico was testing me. In relief and again in repose, I took a breather. While sitting, I heard a scuffling in the small trash receptacle next to me. Since it was adjacent to my throne, I looked inside (stupid of me) and came face to face with a four-and-a-half-inch cucaracha, who was hanging on the edge of the trash can staring up at me. I could see his tentacles feeling the air for the vibrations of the seismic explosion, which had just passed through the room. I swear to you, this may or may not be true, he said to me with his split mouth apparatus, "Rough night, huh?" At least that was what his Spanish amounted to.

Enough! We gathered together and loaded into the van to disembark on our further odyssey through this mysterious land called Mexico. We were Argonauts in search of adventure. Well, it all sounds great, but the point is, we were happy to just be on the road again. It was now three o'clock. I asked Warren to drive again, and this time stay on 185 to the city of Coatzacoalcos, where the road ended on the Gulf Coast. I drifted off with the assured knowledge we were following the correct road by feeling the bounce of the potholes every five feet. Did I mention, the entire time we traveled 185 across the Isthmus de Tehuantepec, which that region of Mexico is properly called, that we only passed three vehicles the entire night. In total, we had driven between 250 and 300 miles that night, ever so slowly, due to the bugs and animals crossing the road through the jungle. We would be okay now; our gas tank was filled, though our stomachs were empty. Still the town of the coffin makers had shaken our confidence, and we would be more cautious from now on. After two hours, the false dawn was opening up with a sliver of sunlight to the east. We were pulling out of the vacuum of the jungle into a sparsely wooded coastal plain. We were nearing the Gulf of Mexico.

11
CAMPECHE OR BUST
TUESDAY
JUNE 24, 1975

The town of Coatzacoalcos did not exist in 1975, not that you would recognize a town. But we did stop next to a beach with palm trees and hauled out of the bus and ran to the water. I showed the boys the difference of this body of water simply in its color alone (gray blue), and its lack of current energy, being of Gulf Coast rather than an ocean. I'd felt it was no mean feat that we crossed an entire country overnight to witness a sunset on the Pacific and a sunrise on the Gulf of Mexico. That, of course, was how I thought, though these kids are Navajos. Their bewilderment to the meaning of what I found significant was not necessarily the same. They had never traveled, I had. Much would certainly digest in their psyche, months, or even years from now as their own personal spheres of experience expanded in their lifetimes.

After splashing and sizing up this great body of water, we loaded up and continued to Sanchez Magallanes. This was a tiny place where the ferry was located that would take us to Barra de Tupilco, where we would continue up the coast of the Yucatan. Luck was with us, and, of course, a cafe was in service for the ferry passengers. We loaded up on *huevos rancheros* (ranch-style eggs), the Mexican version that changes in every new region we traveled. Eggs, beans, tortillas, and a coastal version of *pico de gallo* (rooster's beak) were hitting the spot, and we loaded up with two or three breakfasts each. This was our first meal since Oaxaca, which was noon the previous day. We, of course, indulged in a coastal version of Mexican coffee and were not disappointed, it was just superb.

The ferry was an hour's wait when we finished breakfast. We didn't mind. The morning was beautiful, so we just lounged around and observed an adobe brickmaker working next to where the ferry would land. None of us at this time had ever seen adobe bricks actually being made. Navajos did not build with these; they used logs or railroad ties for their hogans. So, witnessing the process was a worthwhile use of our time. There, of course, was mixed mud in a pile. Then there was straw, chopped with a machete, in another pile. The brickmaker had just finished stomping straw into the pile of mud. While we watched, he shoveled the mud into two-by-four wooden frames the size of his bricks. When these forms were filled, he took another long two-by-four and drew it across the brick frame to level these units. Leaving this alone, he now moved along to another brick frame that had been obviously cast the day before, and he shimmied the frame to release the previous day's creations. From there he moved bricks from another previous day and stood these bricks on end to dry in the sunshine. It was all done in a systematic coordinated harmony that made you appreciate the simplicity of the act. It was quite beautiful to witness this achievement of human ingenuity that at this time in history was responsible for 80% of all human building occupancy on this planet.

The ferry finally showed up. It was a simple affair of a flat-topped barge with a side conning tower to control the vessel. This ferry's platform could handle ten vehicles at a time. It was not much, but it was evident this was not a normal route for most local Natives. There were only three vehicles waiting to board the vessel, and we were the first. The simple ramp was quite adequate for our embarkment. Once parked, thanks to the deckhand who guided us in, we unloaded from the van and stood by the railings to observe the water as we cruised on northeast to Barra de Tupilco.

In my foolish exhaustion, I decided I needed to trust the boys more and give them a daily allowance, which they could use for their meals and any incidentals they saw fit. Learning to use pesos would force them to socialize with the locals. The results of this positively intended economic lesson of independence for the students would come back to bite me in ways expected and unexpected.

From Tupilco, we continued along the coastal road to an intersection north of Sarat. Here we joined the Route 180, which would eventually lead us to our furthest planned destination, Merida. There were again more ferries, but mostly it was bridges to cross on our trek northeast. We crossed the Rio San Pedro and next was the crossing at Cuidad del Carmen, which led straight up a narrow Isla to Puerto Real.

I dozed off after Warren and I switched drivers. Elvis Natan, our trusty sidekick, decided to use the AM radio in the VW van and turned it on. Expecting mariachi music, which would be the norm, we instead discovered sweet calypso music of all things. But why not, we were driving towards the Caribbean. The music was upbeat, lifted our spirits, and was the only source of entertainment this region had offered so far. I glided in and out of consciousness as we cruised up the coast. I was exhausted.

We passed Sabancuy and then further on Chenkan. At Champoton, we stopped for an early dinner, here I doled out pesos to the boys for the next two days' allowance. They would order, through me, what they wanted to eat. I caught Chee and Leon trying to order *cervezas* (beer) and cancelled it.

All total we had used four ferries and a few bridges to get this far. All this took time. From Oaxaca to here felt like a week, but in actuality it was thirty-two hours. At one of the longest ferry waits, we all jumped into our gym shorts (what represented our total swimming apparel) and went swimming in one of the inland bays. I was fascinated to see a couple of the boys had some semblance of an idea of the act of swimming, but how? Had they seen a movie in Gallup and observed maybe Tarzan swimming? Who knows, but they were not afraid of the water in the least bit. They were obviously relishing the experience. There was a great joy in this act. When we were done, we jumped in the van in our wet suits and moved on to the arriving ferry. This was a needed break in a most certainly continuing endless day.

Following dinner in Champoton, we continued to our end of this stretch's destination, Campeche. Tomorrow, hopefully, we would rest.

On the southwest side of town as we entered Campeche, we finally found a walled hotel of sorts. Most likely it had been a *convento* (convent) a hundred years ago. It most certainly had that post clerical vibe much of Mexico still possessed ever since Benito expelled the Catholic Church from its vast ridiculous holdings, which also contributed to the poverty of this nation. The hotel looked safe, and there was a guarded parking lot for the van. We checked in. Finding our three rooms, we immediately relaxed, and I ran for our room's *bano* (bathroom) and settled into nest for a spell. My time spent at these long intervals were becoming more than apparent.

Finally, Warren mentioned I must have the "Revenge!" Resisting hearing this from him, he laughed at me and said "You have Moctezuma's Revenge, all you white guys get it. You just can't handle the water."

To this I responded, "Right" and didn't elaborate any further useless details to validate his hypothesis.

We were all victims of total exhaustion and were essentially now the Walking Dead. Tim was already asleep, then Warren went down. I was the last one standing, and as I inevitably drifted off, but something felt off. In my drifting sleep, our room was in a kind of fuzzy mist, but the strangest thing was the huge rattle and a small man shaking it. It sounds crazy, but he had jade ear plugs, a feather headdress with plumes, which reached the ceiling. He wore an elaborate mantle covering his lower area, but his legs were clear with elaborately decorated sandals of exotic design. He also wore a gold necklace mantle which hung from his neck and covered his chest. It was huge and magnificent. I don't know how he stood under the weight of it. None of this impressed me as much as the furious look of venal hate focused on my own person. "What the hell did I do to you?" All I heard in return was a grunt, a mumble and that damned rattle. Jesus, I needed sleep.

Campeche Fortress Tower

12
SPANISH FORTS
WEDNESDAY
JUNE 25, 1975

That morning, we slept in, Lord, we needed it. Our *convento* (convent) hotel had a small breakfast service, and we were able to eat the local version, of again, *huevos rancheros* (ranch-style eggs). But here the beans were black, contrary to the pinto beans we were used to. Still the meal was quite adequate and recharged our batteries somewhat. Our past journey through the Isthmus had stripped us of a lot of our reserves, and we would need time to rebuild our stamina. This would be a day of easy touring and rest. Midweek in Campeche was perfect. Since we had no weekenders to contend with, the city was all ours.

Campeche was founded in 1540 by Don Francisco de Montejo. It became one of the foremost cities of New Spain in the mid-16th century. There are many buildings of that period in the old San Francisco section of town. The conquest of the Yucatan itself, was made possible by Campeche's proximity. Later, 1.5 miles of hexagonal wall was erected with eight fortresses, due to repeated sackings by pirates in the 16th and

17th centuries. The fortresses and their museums would be our focus that day, so that is what we did.

The day was an adventure. The old Spanish forts were a boy's dream come true. We climbed the bastions, climbed the towers, and tracked the walls of this once formidable fortification. The stonework was now 400 years old and still sustaining an impregnable visage. Heck, we were impressed. We gave the old fort extra points for being everything a kid needed to imagine cannon fire to and fro against marauding pirate fleets. This whole experience alone was worth the entire trip. Afterward, we grabbed some tacos at the complex's entrance. They were great, and, of course, they were followed down with *refrescos* (sodas). These students knew they were being spoiled because sodas were a treat at home. Only at the trading post were they available to them, and the local Ramah café was seldom an opportunity to a poor Navajo boy.

At this point in the day, Edgar White asked if we could go swimming again. Well, why not, so we hauled into the van and started up the coast. It was soon obvious something was different about the water of Campeche proper. There was a foul tinge to the water close to the shore. It was polluted. The city divested its foul sewage, at this time, directly into the open waters adjacent to it. We could not swim here in any of this fecality. We would have to discover a beach with clean blue waters. We continued up the coast and eventually came upon a public beach fulfilling our needs. Since it was a Wednesday, we were its only attendees.

It was a great afternoon; the boys had the wide-open Gulf of Mexico with a subtle confluence of the Caribbean currents affecting the waters with light movement. This was a comfortable, easy body of water and perfect for the desert boys and me. We languished in the easy afternoon's breezes and finally relaxed. We had earned this.

Time had passed quickly. We were realizing the sun was waning, and maybe we should get back to town. For some reason the dark was descending faster than usual. But as a result, we saw what appeared to be a carnival, all lit up, and beckoning visitors. There were small rides and games of all sorts. Most importantly, there was food. Except for maybe one or two of the boys who may have made it to the State Fair in Albuquerque, I don't believe any of these boys knew what a carnival was about.

Warren and I agreed to this diversion and decided to split the boys in two parts, so we could hopefully keep track of them, but first we ate buttered corn on the cob, *hamburguesas* (hamburgers), *chicharones* (deep-fried pork skin), *churros* (deep-fried dough), and cotton candy. The boys all had their allowance now and could purchase what they liked and off we went to explore the carnival of Campeche. You could say this was a treat, but what a better learning experience combined with some fun to boot. This was a good thing.

Elvis and three others were with me. We strolled through the grounds to the different booths displaying food and games, and the boys indulged in whatever frivolity the carnival had to offer. One booth was a target shooting concern that displayed ten-penny nails sitting on a horizontal board. The nails sat on their flat ends erect, and the booth within was packed with huge, plaster castings of crosses and Jesus and Mary and Joseph sculptures painted in hot, Dayglo colors. This was 1975 in Mexico after all. All things considered, here, this was high art. On a lark, I paid the fee of the contest and was handed a short pellet rifle. My first three shots of the ten allowed, missed, but I had gauged the gun sight's flaw and took the next seven nails without a pause. I was given a thirty-inch-tall painted plaster cross, and the boys yelped in surprise. I followed up, now that I knew the site's redundancy, with three more prizes of much larger girth and size. We had the entire Holy Family now, Mary, Joseph, and Jesus, all in Dayglo colors no one in a cemetery could miss. Did I ever mention I was a crack shot on stationary targets? No?

In time we met up and decided we were quite ready to return to the hotel. We had done it all at the carnival, and the Sandman was now beckoning. We loaded up the cross and Holy Family on the laps of the boys and made it back to our new home. We placed all my trophies in our room and stared in wonder as to what the hell Shows was going to do with them. Oh well, it was sack time, so Warren and I got everybody finally bedded down. We'd had a great day.

For some reason I was not tired and wondered if Warren was either. He said, "No, he wasn't."

So, I asked him if we should consider grabbing a beer around the corner for a break.

Warren said, "Why not, everyone else is asleep; right?"

So, after discussing it with Tim Maria, our trusty Lieutenant, we decided, what the heck.

Around the block from our *convento* (convent) hotel was a convenient cantina. It even looked respectable. Warren and I cruised in and sat ourselves down in a small booth and ordered *dos cervezas* (two beers) "Superior" from a handy bartender, who was also serving tables. Earlier on my first trip to Mexico with a fellow teacher, Jesse O'Leary, I had discovered I had a fondness for this particular beer brand. It was a true pilsner with that exotic unique taste only those old German brewmasters, living in Mexico and blending native varieties of grains and hops, could achieve. Warren approved of the taste, and the first one went quickly down our gullets. We were thirsty to say the least.

Soon, we settled down into a comfortable camaraderie, the result of managing seven high school boys in a foreign country with no true compass of destination or expectations. We were winging it. Don't get me wrong, it was still an exciting thrill ride, all in all. But I don't think our expectations of the responsibilities involved were truly thought through. We, I, was responsible for the lives and welfare of seven young Native individuals. "Bring 'um back alive, Andy," was the echoing in my head.

Anyway, we ordered another pair of beers and started talking and comparing notes. Keep in mind, Warren was Navajo and overheard everything going on in the van as we traveled this country. With the beer loosening his tongue, I soon learned that Chee Dodge was up to his antics of sewing discord within the group. This, I was not surprised by. It was a continuation of his behavior of nearly every single day at school. Chee's boredom created havoc. It was just his nature, along with being the world's greatest comedian. But what I didn't know was that he was extorting Warren, himself, with threats of telling parents lies about his behavior during this trip. The fact, that he addressed these threats in front of the other student passengers in the van, made this a serious situation. I stated this to Warren, and he said he understood, but he didn't know if he was even going to continue teaching in adult education. So, ignoring Chee seemed more effective. I knew this was not a solution, but it was apparent to me, Warren was a real nice guy and non-confrontational. There was nothing changing that. I would now have to take on the role of the heavy from now on. Any disciplinary action was going to be my unfortunate task, great.

On our third beer, Warren said he wanted my advice on a particular subject, a woman.

Oh boy, I thought, who was I to give advice about women. They were the more highly evolved level of my species and as comprehensible as the idea of counting the stars in the Milky Way. So, I said to Warren, "Sure, who is she?"

"Beanie," he said.

I was floored, "Really?" I said.

"Yeah," says he. Warren then filled me in on a four-month romance with the infamous Beanie.

She, being an elementary school teacher loved by one and all, was an incredibly generous soul who taught with her heart in her hand. The kids loved her. I could actually see these two together. Warren was a gentle soul himself.

Warren also told me that Beanie had told him she had never experienced these feelings about someone like him before. Warren was smitten, but also concerned, since Beanie was a *Belagaana* (white person), and in 1975, this was still a problem for traditional Navajos.

What could I tell him? I'm a Bellagaana (white person). I asked him if he thought he loved her. He said he thought so, and besides the sex was very loving.

This was where my conscience started interfering along with that third beer. You see, Beanie was very generous with her womanly favors, and many of us knew this. She worked very hard, and it appeared sex was one of her relaxation modes. Add that to the fact she really liked men, and you had a direct representative of the "Free Love" campaign of the late sixties. Should I say anything else in reference to this, hell no! These two might actually be in love and need each other. As a result, I kept my mouth shut, a monumental task, by the way, and wished him luck. Beanie was aces in my book. The *Bellagaana* (white person) thing, was a whole different discourse.

Warren asked if I had a girlfriend, and I said yes. Our relationship was a long-distance complication, which now didn't seem to have a clear future to it, but we were trying. I told him her name was Maria, and she was an ER nurse in Las Vegas, New Mexico. It was a four-hour drive one way just to see her. It was hard. We shook our heads, and suddenly realized it was near one o'clock in the morning, time to leave.

We strolled back to our *convento* (convent). It was a beautiful seaside night with stars twinkling and the sound of the surf carrying far enough to be heard over the quiet, sleepy city. It was the perfect ending to a perfect day. Then we got to the parking lot of the hotel and found Tim Maria waiting for us. "What's up, Tim?" we said.

"Where have you been for so long?" he asked.

"We told you we were going to get a couple of beers. We thought you'd be asleep by now," I said.

Tim then informed us he had been awakened by screaming and then later shouts of *Policia* (Police). He had gotten dressed and checked the rooms and found Chee Dodge and Leon were missing. Following where the screams had come from, he found them hurrying back from the back of the hotel and discovered they were being peeping Toms to the manager's daughters in their private residence. Shit, we were screwed.

Sobering up within seconds, I told Warren to get the boys packed quickly. We had to escape before the cops showed up, otherwise, we might be living in Mexico for a few years longer than expected. I grabbed the two knuckleheads, Chee and Leon, marched to their room and told them they had less than a minute to gather their things and get to the van or they could stay and go to jail. Remarkably, they moved at warp speed. Miraculously, we were in the van and on the road in less than three minutes. We left the parking lot and pulled onto the main avenue fifty feet ahead of a Campeche police car that pulled in after us.

I gunned the van, as much as you can gun a VW Microbus loaded with nine people, and made as much distance between us and the police as possible. It was nearly two in the morning, and I, again, was not going to get any sleep, great. Still, we were not in jail, so we had that going for us. Damn Chee Dodge and his sidekick Leon. This was getting old.

The only reason I could imagine the police didn't proceed to put out an APB on us was obviously because when they checked the rooms for us perpetrators, they found a plaster cross and the whole Holy Family in our room, looking over them with those Dayglo colors you could see in the dark. Don't you think this certainly must have influenced their decision not to apprehend us, don't you? Whatever happened, we escaped, and I don't think the Holy Family hurt our situation the least bit. I hope those girls were happy with Jesus, Mary and Joesph, because we were not coming back.

13
MERIDA BOUND
THURSDAY
JUNE 26, 1975

We were all exhausted. By now the rest of the boys knew what Chee and Leon had done. The bravado of the two did not displace the fact they were sneaky little shits and had almost gotten the whole crew rehoused in a filthy Mexican jail. Of course, they claimed it was all a misunderstanding, which meant, we all understood, that the two of them couldn't be trusted with anything. Still, the tribal thing held, and like it or not they were ours, for better or worse.

Warren and I were wrecks. Not from the three beers, which we never indulged in again after this catastrophe, but from a complete lack of any sleep that night. The two of us were running on empty, and now we were also aware our van's gas tank was again low on petrol. We just couldn't seem to catch a break. There was no alternative, and as always, we just kept driving. Warren and I were tag driving by the half hour at this point. That was all we were capable of. The few minutes rest in between these shifts was not nearly enough to recharge ourselves.

We were fortunately following Route 180 which had been our previous coastal route, but it also continued on through the jungle up the peninsula directly to Merida itself. Escaping Campeche had been easy since this had been the main artery through the city itself.

The further north we drove, the denser the jungle became. Much of the Yucatan is still dense jungle, and Lord knows what lost cities are still hidden in its depths. We now felt we were once again trapped in the Isthmus, the bugs, bats, nighthawks, all of this was still just a short memory away. There were things crawling across the road we couldn't even identify if they were from this planet. None of this boded well with Warren and me. At least the boys, leaning on each other's shoulders, were passed out from their night's fatigue. When would this end?

Tenabo was a village and an intersection of a provincial route onto 180. Here there was a Pemex gas station, and we were saved. On the map, I became happily aware we would be traveling through the more developed sections of the Yucatan. This would not be a repeat of the Isthmus, which no one in their right mind would inhabit. This would be a combination of slash and burn farmland and jungle. There would most certainly be people, and they most likely would be the Maya. This was their part of Mexico and had always been, no matter what the government said. We filled up and those brave souls who dared to use the *banos* (bathrooms), stumbled to this unknown entity. I was eventually in there myself for at least fifteen minutes, and only left due to a concern I might be charged a rental fee. Again, we had survived our own self-inflicted complications and were ready to continue our odyssey into ancient Aztlán. May fortune favor us.

The dawn was cracking through the dense jungle. We were a little revived, and like it or not, ready to continue. Something I failed to mention earlier were the birds. Whether it was due to the high bug concentration or just a total lack of traffic through the jungle, the birds continually flew directly into our microbus from all angles. There was nothing we could do but continue to drive. Still, parakeets, parrots of all types, and many other exotic species persisted in their collisions into our moving vehicle. This was so disturbing. There were also small dents on the van body where larger birds, chasing some meal or other, slammed into us. That is how pristine this jungle was in 1975. We were an unexpected reality.

Warren and I somehow continued driving. I don't know how we did it. I've always thought having no alternative is one of the surest ways to success. We made it to Calkini later that morning and discovered a cantina-cafe willing to serve this tribe of Navajos and the *blanco* (white person). The eggs and beans were great, and there was also fruit: mangoes, papaya, even pineapple. This was something the boys had not engaged in as far as their dietary explorations were concerned. Ah, brave new worlds, a few of them took to this culinary offering enthusiastically. Who knew?

Following breakfast, we loaded into the van and proceeded on to our destination, Merida. The weather was good. Truthfully, we had not had a cloudy day since we started, just bright sunny days. We continued through the towns of Halacho, Maxcanu, and as we neared Uman, I became aware that our brakes were feeling spongy. Considering that descension off the continental plateau south of Oaxaca with the weight of nine individuals pressing on those brake pads for two hours, I was not the least bit surprised. Maybe we should try to exchange vehicles at another agency, if there was one, and if they also had another microbus. Oh well, we were fine for now.

As we were nearing Merida, the largest city in the Yucatan and the capital of the province, we were driving through much of the outlier city with narrow lanes and busy pedestrian and residential occupation. Everything seemed fine, except that this van of ours contained nine exhausted human bodies in desperate need of rest. It was nearing sundown. We had been driving all day, and maybe we were travelling faster now that the goal of a hotel and food was within reach. A small child, a girl of let's say four, stepped into the narrow lane where we were traveling. I hit the brakes, I hit them again, and somehow, besides the fact of our momentum, we impossibly halted. We had all been thrown forward in the lurch but were okay. The child was one foot from our bumper and screaming. Hell, I'd be screaming that close to death also. The absent mother appeared out of nowhere, and I'm sure out of the horror of what could have occurred, started shouting and cursing in Spanish. I'm certain the relief of the situation spurred her need to expound this unknown part of the Spanish dictionary to us. The little girl was okay, we were okay, but the brakes were not. This would be a priority in our stay in Merida.

Thanks to our travel guide from the car agency in Mexico City, we identified a suitable hotel in the name of Hotel Margarita. This lodging filled the bill, and we were instantly grateful in its location and ambience. The place was great. Secured parking was available and after unloading the eight Navajo refugees from Campeche, I parked. There, upon settling in and with what energy was left in our bodies, we made our way to a nearby cafe, pointed out by the hotel's night clerk. Too tired to even remember what we ate, it was something, we dragged ourselves back to our rooms and literally crashed and burned. There was no reason to be concerned about a repeat of the night before's performance since the boys were now essentially DOA in Merida.

I settled my exhausted buns on this throne of Merida and delivered my assessment of the last 24 hours. It took some time. Then collapsing onto my bed, behind my closed eyes, I felt a sudden falling sensation. This was probably the helplessness, the after reaction, to the nearly taking of a small girl's life. But no, it wasn't. I heard the rattle again, clear as a bell, and there he stood, in his feathered magnificence—this was Moctezuma, at least according to Warren. He was even angrier than before, or was he always angry? What did I know? He shook and raised his arms and made some kind of incantation or curse toward me, threatening, with that damned rattle. "Well hell, I appreciate your concern but after Campeche, I need some sleep, so good night."

14
HOME OF THE CONQUISTADORS
FRIDAY
JUNE 27, 1975

Merida was a Spanish colonial city. It was not like other places in Mexico. Merida was a mixture of modern, timeless, and international all wrapped into one loosely contained society of people from, and immigrated to, this immense northern section of the Yucatan. Not only was it the capital city, but it was also the major conduit of present-day civilization into this ancient labyrinth of jungle and ruins, which makes up this eastern-most section of Mexico. In all truth, the Yucatan is actually a hidden mystery of lost cities and cultures that mankind will be exploring for centuries to come.

The morning after the escape from Campeche, we gathered in the Hotel Margarita's lobby late and made our way to the same cafe that had served us the night before. Warren and I had decided to return the van. Since we discovered there was a rental dealership here, we would get us some new wheels. Also, another trip to the Banco Nacional would be necessary since banks were a rare commodity in Mexico, and we needed cash to continue. When breakfast was done, I informed the boys they would be writing in their diaries this morning, and Tim Maria would be overseeing them. It would take some time for me and Warren to get all of our errands squared away, but with these kids as exhausted as we still were, I didn't foresee any problems. Once back at the hotel, we had our crew settled in, and off we went in search of Eldorado, or at least a few more pesos and a new van with fresh brakes.

Thanks to the city map the car rental agency had given us in Mexico City, we were fortunate to discover the agency was not too, too far. After a little hoofing, we found it. Again, with grace and accommodation, we were treated quite well, and there appeared to be no problems for the automobile exchange. It felt to me like a normal process in this business since Mexico was so vast and often brutally primitive, at this time, as far as roads were concerned. The nature of the jungle alone seemed to necessitate a relief pony or car along the way in order to reach your destination. Any travel was an adventure in this country of many contradictions.

We left the rental dealership with a new-feeling VW Microbus. It had a white top and blue bottom. It was clean, ran well, and the brakes were back to a normal response to your foot's demand. Our spirits were recharged at the sight of it. This was our new war pony who would get us back to Mexico City when we were ready to depart.

The bank was also no problem, thank God, it was Friday, and we cashed a number of checks for funds we would need to continue our odyssey through Aztlán. With our morning shot, Warren and I returned to the hotel and gathered up our chicks and strode off into the midday sun in search of the city's *zocalo /plaza* (square). Hopefully we might find some lunch, a concept which had often escaped us in our run through the uncertain circumstances of this adventure. Things were looking up. Everyone reflected a cheerfulness not apparent in quite a while. Maybe through this journey there was some, just some, maturing taking place. One could only hope.

Later, thanks to friendly directions, we walked to the city's *mercado* (market). We marched together, this motley crew of nine Navajos in straw cowboy hats and one tall, awkward *gringo* (white person). Yes, we got stares, but why not? We certainly weren't locals. Maybe the local populace thought we were a new gang moving into virgin territory, who knows? Arriving at the market, it was crowded and fascinating. I know the boys had no concept of what a *mercado* (market) was in the real sense. Our trading post was our *mercado* (market), though really, it was not a fair comparison, not at all.

While walking through the market, I was explaining to the boys this *mercado* (market) was around 450 years old, and generations of families had either shopped or sold produce here. This kind of concept of time was incomprehensible to a boy from a nomadic society where time was fluid and always moving. Within this institution of universal commerce for the basic necessities of human survival, there was every conceivable item for sale here. Fruits and vegetables, of course, a bounty in the aisles, along with cages of live chickens and turkeys, filled our vision throughout. There were cages of parakeets and finches for sale, a rainbow within themselves in colors you could only dream of. Vendors of leather goods with belts and wallets were everywhere. You could even get hardware of every tool or nail or toilet plunger you would ever need. This *mercado* (market) was a cornucopia of all of societies' domestic necessities. Ask a vendor for something you would consider an obscure request, and he or she could direct you to whosoever would be selling that particular item a few booths away. This was all so amazing, and the boys were mightily impressed.

Since we had been to the bank, I was able to dole out the agreed daily allowance in pesos, and as a result, Warren and I split the boys up and went shopping. There really wasn't anything we could use on the road, but you never knew. The joy of just being part of this most ancient of societal interactions in commerce, the *mercado* (market), was immensely satisfying and exciting.

Somehow, I remembered a story that the Maya would tell of a most beloved old grandmother, who, after a long life, found herself inevitably at death's door. While laying on her bed and being visited for the last time by friends and family with their final goodbyes, she heard a comment about the market. In her struggling deathly throes, she whispered ever so softly, "What day is this?"

In considerable shock, those who were gathered said, "It is Friday, of course, why do you ask?"

At this and everyone's astonishment, the old woman opened her eyes and said out loud, "It's market day!" And with that, she got off her deathbed, dressed in her shawl, picked up her bag, and ran off to the *mercado* (market). The story is ancient and still could be included in any story of human civilization on this planet. Yet, as everyone knows, nothing stops a determined woman from the most important social event ever invented—shopping!

Miraculously, the scouting parties met up and appeared none the worse for wear. There were even some smiles amongst them, wow! Collectively, we then snaked our group through the still busy market and eventually found the entrance where we had first arrived. Thanks to that fact, we knew where we were. From here we marched to the *plaza* (square) to see the historic sites of this major center of Merida.

As we were walking to the *plaza* (square), I suddenly had to acknowledge my body was not up to snuff. I felt fatigued, just worn out, all of a sudden. I had to accept that my nightly visits from Moctezuma were draining me. I knew the frustration of trying to keep the boys entertained, as well as disciplined for their own protection, was more than I ever expected, but hell, I was a 24-year-old "Know it all." I deserved what I got. Who else in their right mind would have placed themselves in this situation? But I digress, this was my own self-inflicted conundrum, oh well.

We approached the Plaza de la Independencia as it was known, and it became apparent for the first time that the city was bustling with numbers of people we had not witnessed before. Merida was hopping. This *plaza* (square) was impressive in a way we had not seen before. It never dawned on us this place would attract all of the Yucatan as well as boatloads of Europeans who were attracted to the weather, relaxed atmosphere, and most of all, the significant archaeological finds that this interior hemisphere had to offer. There was another quite unusual occurrence that became apparent at this time. We observed many blonde Mexicans, well, Spaniards really, as far as descendancy. These individuals were obviously the spawn of the conquistadors, still segregating themselves in their self-sustained exceptionalism from the main population of this country. It was obvious who they thought and knew they were, and they let everyone else know it as well. After 450 years they were still trying to conquer the Yucatan with their blonde hair.

The *Palacio del Gobierno* (Palace of the Government), we had discovered on our rental car map, was our first visit into the culture of this jungle capital. Though the physical architecture, in fabulous Moorish and European accents, was magnificent, centuries of use and the brutal humid weather placed the pale of a tired old appearance one could not avoid. Still, in the upper ballroom Orozco's murals were in attendance and beyond impressive. The murals themselves were taking a beating in this humid atmosphere but were standing strong to share the artist's message of the right to revolution of an oppressed people.

After the *Palacio* (palace) we had tacos on the plaza and were entertained by an organ grinder and his spider monkey. The monkey took to the students, and it was good to see them interact in a childlike innocent way with a simple tree monkey from the local jungle. This event contributed to an especially good lunch. There were people everywhere. It turns out that this was Merida's peak season, and Warren and I were now aware getting rooms at Hotel Margarita had been simply dumb luck. Thank you, Jesus.

Saying goodbye to the monkey and his pet grinder, we now searched for the Municipal Museum. Expecting artifacts representing the magnificent excavations surrounding Merida, we instead found old worn-out displays of the city's progress in development through the centuries. It was obvious the great wealth, accumulated by legacies of the conquistadors and old generals and land barons, would never be overshadowed by the Indios whose ancient foundations this new wealth was founded upon. The Indios were okay in their fields of sisal fiber, but their legacies and contributions were blatantly removed from the municipal reality. They were not included in 1975 in this rich capital of affluence and cosmopolitan celebration. They were the shadows of this city that thrived due to their endurance.

After the museum, we walked the *plaza* (square). I pointed out unusual street performers and the historical buildings with beautiful aspects worth photographing. There was no clue as to what the boys were actually recording on film. It was just assumed they would be focused on the physical dynamics of the trip. Time would tell if they took some of my advice, if any. Our erratic journey had interrupted much of the planned diary recording of the boys. This would hopefully improve now that Chee and Leon had finally settled down, we prayed.

The remainder of the day rolled by quickly. Suddenly the sun was waning toward the west, and the town's population of locals and visitors were taking their leave of this pleasant day in this charming setting. The whole gang was hungry. This included me, and the condition my condition was in was depleting my physical reserves most rapidly. As soon as we could, we found a simple café-cantina and ordered the local version of a combination plate *de Mexicana* (of Mexico). The food was simple and good but still could not compete with our own *Nuevo Mexicano* (New Mexican) fare.

As dinner was ending, Warren and I reviewed with the boys the possibility of continuing traveling further southeast to Chetumal, next to the Belize border. From there we could make a straight shot across Route 186 west to Francisco Escarsega and then back to Mexico City. No one objected, and I was feeling a sense of relief there had been no more disturbances to our travel plans. Maybe with a false sense of optimism, I proposed the next day, Saturday, to be a kind of morning off for everyone. Once they had received their allowance after breakfast, all would be allowed to explore the city on their own until one in the afternoon, then they would meet at the old clock on the *plaza* (square) that we had discovered on the first day. From there we would proceed to lunch and compare adventures. It all sounded so great. What could go wrong?

That night after bedding the gang down and talking over the new route east to Chetumal with Warren, I collapsed into bed. There had been a particularly dissipating episode at our fountainhead throne for me. The exhaustion and fatigue of my physical punishment were starting to get the best of me. Would this ever end? Eventually, with the awareness of my desperate situation finally fading into sleep, again he appeared. "What ta' hell!" He was holding two huge viciously wreathing rattlesnakes; I'm not talking babies either. Their heads were the size of my fists. I could hear that damn background rattling even though he held no rattles. Moctezuma just danced in front of me poking those squirming, killing machines in my direction. Was there a point to this demonstration? Was there a message? Hell if I knew! After the draining fatigue I had experienced this ever-eternal day, I passed out in a painful delirium and slept in a deep death sleep with dreams you would not wish on anyone of consequence.

15
THE RAZOR'S EDGE
SATURDAY
JUNE 28, 1975

The noise of the city woke us with car horns honking, people shouting in the street, and conversations carried on the too-rare occurrence of a breeze to our rooms. This sudden shift in the city's daily life could only mean one thing, it was Saturday, and everyone was coming to town. This was the people's day to shop and socialize from the distant outskirts of the city, from small villages and farms. There would be gatherings on the *plaza* (square), including birthday celebrations and family reunions, and anything that would permit a joining of friends in celebration.

The boys joined me and Warren downstairs in the lobby, and I doled out pesos for their day's adventure into the culture of the Yucatan. We did find some tables at our most recent favorite cafe on the plaza first and had breakfast. As we awaited its delivery, we observed some traditionally dressed Meridans perform what they called the Belt Dance. It appears the city sponsored dances on the weekends for the tourists, probably in anticipation of questions of non-inclusivity of the local Native populations. Either way, it was a wonderful addition to our Saturday adventure.

After breakfast everyone scattered. This was the first time they had been cut loose. Please God, look after them, they have to grow up sometime.

This morning, I had noticed for the first time that Orlando and Cooper Eriacho had pale palors to them, and for a Navajo that was extremely unusual. At breakfast, I had also noticed they were not eating. I prayed whatever bug was bothering them would release them soon. Outside of that, they seemed fine and strolled off to follow the others in exploration.

Warren and I walked the *plaza* (square) and side streets, discovering any number of diversions. During this time, we also discussed the route to Chetumal on the Caribbean coast. We agreed the road to Valladolid would connect us with Route 295 which would then take us to Felipe Carrillo Puerto, this being the largest city on the eastern side of the Yucatan. From Felipe south to Route 307, we would run straight for Chetumal. It was a sound plan, and we felt secure in the directions.

After strolling and touring for a while, eventually it became obvious it was about a half an hour before the meet, and we should start moving towards the rendezvous spot. As soon as we approached the old clock, we saw Tim Maria.

He was frantically marching up and down the sidewalk. When he caught sight of us, he ran toward us. "Where the heck have you been? Chee Dodge is going to be killed."

Oh shit. I thought, what now? Tim had us follow him, at a run, two blocks off the plaza to a very small barber shop with a tiny barber pole in the window. What was happening on the street in front of the barber shop was terrifying. The barber, all of five foot two and probably about eighty, had a straight razor to Chee's throat and was holding him hostage. All the while this was happening, Leon, who could barely stand up, was pushing the barber and in Navajo spoken so drunkenly even a Navajo couldn't understand him, was threatening him.

These two derelicts, Chee and Leon, had obviously taken their pesos and found a bar, probably as soon as they left from breakfast. They had been drinking all morning and probably stumbling out of the bar later, broke. Chee eyed the barber shop and decided he needed a haircut. How the hell they even communicated with the barber was an incredible miracle in itself, but not remembering they were broke, was certainly their downfall.

As I approached the barber, I was careful to be as conciliatory towards him as I could. I explained to him I was these two knucklehead's teacher and asked what the problem was. All of this was carried out in the most embarrassing strung together group of nouns and adjectives the poor Spanish language should ever have to endure. I was pathetic, but somehow the old man looked at me with his rheumy old eyes and explained this little shit had not paid him for his haircut, and he was too old to tolerate this abuse. All this time, the razor never left Chee's throat through the entire discourse. And Chee, good old Chee, I don't know how he was even standing up he was so drunk, to add to these desperate negotiations and all during this time, he was mouthing off to the barber and egging Leon on to a final showdown, Jesus. His excuse for not paying was, he didn't like the haircut rather than the fact he had no money.

Suddenly, the old barber starts shouting *policia* (police). Oh great, I pleaded with the barber and finally pulled out a wad of pesos. There was no time to negotiate. The old man took the money, lowered the razor. As I and Warren and Tim Maria dragged the boys away, he raised the razor in the air in threatening gestures. In my miniscule ability to interpret, I believe he was offering a "final shave" to all of us if we ever came this way again.

I won't lie, this event changed everything. Even as Chee and Leon denied everything, I knew they were threatening our odyssey. We had traveled too far for trouble to take us now. I couldn't risk the lives of the remaining seven of us to a final disaster these two would orchestrate to befall us. This incident had scared the hell out of me. I was now afraid and felt it was time to retreat from our future plans.

When we got back to the *plaza* (square), all the remaining students were in attendance and were in a state of expectation. They obviously knew what Chee and Leon would be up to, and I, in my oblivious optimistic attitude, was not the least bit able to reckon the reality of these two outlaws' havocs. Everyone knew how upset I was. I was having a hard time keeping control of my emotions. There were two instigators, who at the time, I would be more than willing to eliminate, quite willing. So, with this in mind, it was time to come up with a cooling down remedy for those on the brink of disastrous inclinations, vis-á-vis, myself. Warren and I decided to take the whole gang to the movies. Chee Dodge and Leon, still staggering drunk, were dragged along in our disgust. What else could we do with them, leave them in the room at the hotel? Yeah right, they would probably come to and burn the place down before the movie was over.

Now the movie showing at the *cine* (movie theater) was the last thing I would ever expect to see in Mexico, but why not? "The Exorcist" was shining on the marquee, and Warren asked me what it was about. I explained the film would be good therapy for our two troublemakers, and the others might find it useful as well. The theater's ambiance was that of an old Art Nouveau theme. It was two blocks off the corner of the central plaza and must have welcomed the whole of northern Yucatan through its doors. For a Saturday afternoon, there was a fairly large crowd already seated when we arrived. Finding the last row only half-full in the dark, we shuffled into the seats with Chee and Leon stuck between Warren and myself. They were not going anywhere. Somehow, we had entered the theater in the middle of the previews and special shorts appropriate in Mexico, so this was lucky.

The Exorcist was "The Exorcist!" I had seen the movie probably two years before, but it had finally made it down to Mexico way. I believe the thing that saved the kids from wetting the bed that night was the fact that the movie was dubbed in Spanish at the bottom of the screen, so any audible terror was second hand. While watching the beginning of the movie, just to make our afternoon complete, at the scene of the small girl projecting vomit onto the priest Leon erupted in response in front of himself. Oh great. Warren and I looked at each other. I was at the end of the aisle, so I apprehended our bad boy and dragged him off to the *banos* (bathrooms). Jesus, he could barely stand. We found our way to the *caballeros* (men), and upon opening the door, I almost lost my cookies from the smell. There was a sink, thank God, and I cleaned Leon up enough so that the rest of us would not get sick smelling him.

It was for some reason at this point, I reviewed the fact that I received no salary for this adventure. What I knew now, was that Warren had negotiated a salary that I had no knowledge of back at home before we left. Oh well, it was my plan of exploration, and I was seeing Mexico. At this point though, I decided, Warren could clean up Leon the next time.

The movie eventually ended, and without any more projecting critiques from the peanut gallery, we exited the theater and found a late afternoon of pleasant sunshine and the promenading of the local population on the *plaza* (square). By this time our outlaws had started sobering up, and they were starting to mouth off about how they were being treated. That was enough, we all were fed up with their antics, and in Navajo and English we impolitely told them off. With that, Warren and I later marched our tribe to our favorite cafe and proceeded to order dinner. Since everyone was paying with their allowance, I kept an eye on Orlando and Cooper. They were not ordering, these two looked sick. I asked Warren if he knew what was going on with those two. Warren leaned over to Tim Maria and asked him. After conversing quietly in Navajo for a minute, Warren whispered to me, the two brothers had not eaten since they had been receiving an allowance. They were saving for a Fuzz buster for their electric guitars. There were no jobs or money-making opportunities on our small reservation for teenage boys, so these two had decided this allowance was the only sure possibility to the Holy Grail of rock'n'roll reverberation, the Fuzz buster. They only had-to stay alive and not eat and save this money, that's all.

Jesus F Christ, what else could throw a wrench at me. Right there on the spot, I informed everyone the allowance would cease. If they needed something I would purchase it. From then on, I would be caring for all expenses and that was that. I did include though, an addendum, that before we left Mexico City for home, we would go shopping for anything special they wanted to take home. There was, of course, much grumbling, but after that day's close encounter with disaster, many actually appeared relieved.

On the way back to Hotel Margarita, I spoke to Warren about returning to Mexico City, starting the next day. He saw the wisdom of the proposal, and I believe he might have been more frightened than I from this day's encounters. We were agreed and would pull out early tomorrow morning even though it was Sunday. There is one positive note to add. Cooper and Orlando finally ate enough that their native color was returning. So, their financial hunger strike had finally ended. They would live, besides their best intentions.

We hit the sack early, knowing Sunday would be the longest segment of our trip. The intention was to see Uxmal early in the morning. This was the fabulous round pyramid of the wizard and was not to be missed. After Uxmal, we were shooting straight for Villahermosa, an area that would lead us eventually through oil country, Pemex territory, the life's blood of every city bus and Volkswagen bug running the roads in Mexico.

My continuing ablutions to Moctezuma were vicious that evening. The internal bubbling springs of my intestines reflected the stress and lack of physical fortitude my entire body was denying me. I was shot. Emotionally, I felt I had failed my crew and yet knew if I was to ever get them home alive, our new path was the only chance. Laying my head down finally, my tired bones were slowly collapsing into a restive state. Maybe this climax of our odyssey was my cure. With the decision made for the good of our war band, I might get to sleep the sleep of the just. Oh heck, did I say that? As soon as the thought escaped my frontal cortex, I heard a drum and a rattle sound. There was that indistinguishable chanting sound, the old boy was at it again. In my unconscious vision of twilight dreaming there stood in all his glory, the Emperor Moctezuma. There was probably not a parrot or a Quetzel or other bird of color left in the jungle for all the feathered adornment old "Moc "was wearing. He was beating a gold braided drum loudly and trying to now sing above his own noise. I'd laugh, but he was so serious. What did he want? He knew his curse was in full operation. I'd be lucky to get out of Mexico alive for all the agony. Finally with the drumming driving to a crescendo, I shouted at him, "Enough, stop, do you think you got a raw deal with Cortez, try dealing with my students, Chee Dodge and Leon for just one day and see how you feel." The drumming suddenly stopped, and I gratefully fell off to sleep.

Zocalo Merida

Merida Chapel

16
UXMAL
SUNDAY
JUNE 29, 1975

Grabbing some baked goods from a vendor near the plaza, we proceeded to escape Merida in the early morning hours. All was quiet, it was *Domingo* (Sunday) after all, time for the locals to sober up and go to church. Merida was harder to exit than it had been to enter for some reason. The reverse one-way streets ran amok from pure logic, but eventually we weathered the confusion and escaped the city's vacuum. We found Route 180 and started driving to Uman.

In Uman, Warren and I found Route 261, which would take us to Uxmal. After some steady driving, we were becoming more aware of how jungle farmers grew *maize* (corn). Slash and burn was the accepted technique passed down for thousands of years from the Olmecs to the Toltecs to the Maya and any identifiable Yucatan tribal society. This meant, as we traversed this jungle countryside, often large checkerboard patches of jungle would open up as fields of corn on maturing stocks. As we neared Uxmal about nine-thirty in the morning, we found an archaeological marker on the roadside and followed it past many cornfields to the site of Uxmal. Nothing is stranger than seeing a pyramid in the distance surrounded by *maize* (corn), and yet a thousand years ago this would have been typical.

As we neared the ruin complex, it became apparent this site was no small Mayan endeavor. This was, at one time, a most significant central conduit to all the outlier kingdoms of this section of the Mayan empire. In essence, this was a capital of this region and a thoroughly unique one at that.

We parked the van, got out and were eventually met by a sleepy guard/caretaker of sorts. At that time, without uniforms, he could have been a farmer checking the fields and saw some easy pesos and relieved us of them. Who knew? It was never much, and we were glad to have the whole place to ourselves. We started climbing. The physical state of this complex was mostly rubble. You could see that probably the last five years was spent just releasing the ruins from 800 years of the jungle vegetation that it had been imprisoned in and hidden by.

Still there were relief sculptures of turtles along palace wall friezes. There were skulls carved on the pyramid itself. The pyramid was a round/elliptical, and the only one of its kind. I had somewhere read of the site's mythology concerning a dwarf. Supposedly, he hatched the pyramid from an egg with magical properties. In reality, there were five superimposed structures which made-up the present monument.

The boys climbed all over the pyramid, took pictures of each other, and then proceeded to shout echoes in the empty corridors of the palace halls. They were having a good time. I was glad. Things felt more positive. Eventually, we found ourselves in a small open courtyard just south of what was called on signage "The Nunnery." Here was the ball court of the Mayan games. The large stone game ring was hovering above us still inset in the limestone walls. For a few moments, I explained to the students how no hand could touch the rubber ball when in play, but every other part of the human body could have contact with it. This was no kind of basketball. I explained that in this game, whoever got the ball through the ring could then run into the cheering audience, and whoever he was able to apprehend would have to surrender all his material wealth to him. Thus, the audience must also be in pretty good shape, in order to outrun the victor. It was at this point I noticed, while still listening, some of the boys seemed distracted by something. I stopped my discourse and listened. There was a heavy plodding, rumbling on the earth sound coming from the far end of the ball court. We all turned in that direction to observe dinosaurs making their way across the corridor towards us. There were eight of them, fierce, scaly and with long spiked tails. It just so happened, the boys were witnessing their first iguanas, but not small tree iguanas, these were big fellas, between two and three hundred pounds each. To me they were beautiful, to the boys, "Let's get the hell out of here, *skeego*!" (move it in Navajo), so we left.

Following our quick exit, we had then by happenstance discovered the beak-nosed Chac, the rain god, so we continued to explore almost all the entire site, which was mostly rubble and bare dirt remains. This was once a most fabulous center of the Mayan civilization. Hopefully the archaeologists would make it so again.

It was time to move on. Loading the van with ourselves and this new experience, we took off to continue this long day's journey into night. Following Route 261, we came to the village of Hopelchen. Here we found snacks and food to call lunch, and we also grabbed *refrescos* (sodas) on the way out the door of this Mexican convenience store. We were now facing the longest stretch of our odyssey into Aztlán. Leaving Hopelchen, we drove to the coast to Haltunchen bypassing Campeche and any wanted posters out for us, smart move, huh?

There was a pleasantly unusual event on the way to the coast through the jungle. Somewhere east of Sihochac, we encountered the most beautiful cemetery on the right side of the road, as we were cruising through the forest. A huge field of grave markers freshly painted in whitewash just sprung out at us with fresh and plastic flowers decorating it obviously with love. I hate to say it, but it was nearly inviting. The most amazing aspect of this peculiar phenomenon was that there was an adjacent field where a baseball game was being played on this beautiful Sunday afternoon. Both teams wore uniforms, and it was visually obvious they were young Mayans. The deep green of the jungle contrasting with the white of the uniforms and the colored flowers decorating the graves was a mental snapshot our minds would never forget. Visually, it was magical and the juxtaposition of the two manifestations of our being, one of life, one of death, somehow felt appropriate. This was in actuality, and in reflection, a joyful experience, and all occurring within a slow drive-by viewing.

We continued down Route 201 past Champoton straight to Francisco Escarcega. Here we were able to connect with 186 west, knowing finally this route would take us to our eventual destination of Villahermosa. We crossed the Rio Candelaria and soon after crossed the Rio Usumacinto. The truth is, it wasn't "soon," but I'm trying to pick up the pace of a boring travelogue. Anyway, after the Rio Usumacinto, we were out of the Yucatan and traveling into the oil rich basin past the Bay of Campeche. This became an observational shock to our systems. This was oil country, and that raw exploitation of the earth was in complete opposition to our previous experiences in Mexico. Until now, Mexico was a gracious example of the synergy between man and the land—a trusted bond of existence through the millennia, of man tending the farming landscape in the caretaker role provided him by the earth for his survival.

Nothing was the same moving forward. We passed through many villages and towns, Chable, Catazoja, Chichonal, sister to the city of Macuspans, and were still headed for Villahermosa. Fuel trucks and cars drove very fast here and dangerously. There were many close calls to our little VW Microbus. I held the wheel in an iron grip all the way. It was exhausting. Besides the dangerous drivers, there were wrecks of fuel trucks along the side of the highway. Some were recent and barbecued to a metal mangled crisp. Some were even being reclaimed by the jungle, weeds dragging the remains back to Mother Earth. We all agreed, no one could possibly have survived any of those accidents. The drivers were obviously all goners. Yet, the fuel trucks passed us on risky curving roads at ridiculous speeds beyond any reason. God bless them all, they were going to need it.

By the time we reached the outskirts of Villahermosa, it was way past dark. This was a city of industry, not tourism. Finding a resting place was going to be a challenge. We drove through, we hoped, the central municipal heart of downtown, and were not finding our luck in good standing here. My eyes were bloodshot from the driving because the longest leg of the drive had been mine. Warren had gotten us to Francisco Escarcego when I had taken over.

There appeared a very small sign on the left, suddenly, that said hotel. This place was flush on the road curb and had no parking, but we were out of time, and it would have to do. They did have three rooms, thank God, and told us to park on the street, okay? Grabbing our suitcases and leaving the remainder of our possessions in the bus, we dragged our road-weary bodies through the doors of this sad excuse for a hotel in Villahermosa and just hit the sack.

Oh, the agony and the ecstasy of that night's dreams were unreal. I don't know if it was the ruins of Uxmal or the devastating contrast of the green Yucatan to this dirty petroleum existence called Villahermosa that disturbed my subconscious. He wasn't there in my dreams that night. Maybe it was his day off, but I did hear that thumping drumming of Moctezuma in the background all night long. Was there a message? I wouldn't remember by morning anyway, as the doors of my consciousness closed for the night.

Pyramid of the Wizard
Uxmal Ruins

Pyramid of the Wizard #2 Uxmal Ruins

Mayan Ball Court Ring in Uxmal Ruins

Nunnery at Uxmal Ruins

Nunnery #2 at Uxmal Ruins

17
BANDITOS
MONDAY
JUNE 30, 1975

Waking the next morning to noisy traffic outside our hotel room's window, we were all experiencing a driving hangover from the previous day's demands. Collecting ourselves into some semblance of a cohesive group again, we marched to the van parked on the street outside to depart. Something was wrong. A door to the van was not closed all the way. We had been robbed. The driver's side vent window had been pried open, and the thieves had reached in and unlocked the door. The van was empty. Cooper and Orlando's guitars and all of the other boys accumulated treasures had been stolen. My leather side pack, which contained trip receipts, the boy's diaries, 35mm slide film, and brochures of monuments and museums we had visited, were gone. But the cherry on the top was, they had also stolen our two cameras. There was no joy in Mudville that morning. Casey's bat was probably also stolen. Well, hell, we ran back to the hotel to complain. The desk clerk could do nothing, "Would you like the police?" What good would that do; besides, they might have connections to Campeche.

In anger and frustration, we collected our suitcases, we thanked God, we still had them and marched backed to our abused and violated Volkswagen Microbus and sped out of Villahermosa as quickly as we could make tracks. There was a sense in the group, beyond a resentful grumbling, that this city could travel far into the depths of hell and not a single one of us would mind in the least.

Grabbing some food on the road at a palapa cafe, we continued on Route 185 that eventually got us to Cosoleacaque. A while later we intersected into Route 180 at the village of Jaltipan. About this time, I sensed a grumbling in the tribe. They were disheartened by the theft the previous night and were now in a dejected mood, allowing them to listen to Chee Dodge's complaints that were directed at my leadership and group guidance. I looked at Warren and realized he would be no help. So, I was on my own. Chee complained that I got angry a lot for no reason. He explained that we appeared to be driving all the time instead of stopping and seeing anything. After his Navajo-English dissertation, it was obvious he had a mutiny planned, and these complaints were his first salvos at my leadership. By now, I knew Chee well enough and figured if I left this rebellious display of his continue, he would rile up the whole tribe against me, and I would be toast.

I let him finish his harangue, and then I apologized to all the boys for my recent frustrated angry displays. I then stated that I was responsible for their lives, and getting them back home in one piece and that left me much more tense than when we were safe at home in the classroom. Then I laid into Chee and Leon for all the grief and trouble we had experienced due to their shenanigans. This point was good and bad in relationship to the group. On one hand, we all knew this duo had threatened our security with possible detainment in jail. On the other hand, these were young tribal members who stuck together through thick or thin no matter what. I was not a member of this club and never would be, this fact fogged up the works as far as the obvious right and wrong of this situation was concerned. Now, I was certain, this earlier return trip had been necessary. Chee was working his magic of dissent and discord. I hoped I might have enough time to get everyone back to Mexico City and then on the train back to El Paso, but only time would tell.

Finally, the boys calmed down somewhat, and I told them of my plan to stop in Veracruz for a long rest after our escape from the Yucatan. This appeared to appease the tribal rumbles for the moment, good. We still had a hell of a long drive ahead of us to get there, but there was also much to see in the variety of landscape and villages we passed. We drove through Hueyapan, San Andres, Tuxtla and Santiago Tuxtla. At the latter, we grabbed some tacos from a vendor on the road. The boys were by now too comatose from the driving to even dream of rebellion. Kilometer by kilometer we inched our way towards Veracruz. At Alvarado, those of us who were still awake or aware, witnessed the wildlife of the beautiful Laguna Alvarado. After one more long stretch of road, we saw the outskirts of Veracruz.

We entered the port city's *El Centro* (the center) and miraculously discovered a wonderful portside hotel not far from the shoreline. With secured parking included, not that we now had anything of value anymore, we unloaded our suitcases and checked in. Afterward it was very late, but this crew needed feeding. We found a restaurant not far from our new residence. The amazing thing about Veracruz in 1975 was there were marimbas playing throughout the city. Every restaurant and bar had musicians playing nonstop. It felt like there was a battle of the marimbas playing all through the day and most of the night. It was, without exaggeration, enchanting. As a group, we were charmed. The boys, watching the dexterity of the musicians, found it fascinating. This musical balm was just what the doctor ordered. It calmed our savage hearts and allowed our hunger to direct us to a seafood restaurant that enslaved us with accents of fried garlic, fish, and butter. Heaven was beckoning, bon appetite.

I don't remember what the boys ordered. I had translated, in my sorry interpretation, the Spanish menu for them. Still, all seemed happy with what they got. Funny how the hunger of exhaustion can open your horizons to the possibilities of more varied menu selections. As for myself, I chose the octopus, cooked in its own dye sauce. The boys were disgusted with my selection when it arrived. They had never even seen an octopus before, so just the visual contact with one unnerved them. Out of an amazed fear of the poor thing, they warned me not to eat it, but being a son of Baltimore, I relished every amazing forkful into my mouth's cavity. We ate our fill, and it was well deserved. I felt we had completed our longest treks, and now was the time to rejoice to the success of our survival.

With dinner ending, we strolled through the evening streets of Veracruz. Music was everywhere. The sea breezes coming off the gulf were doing the bidding of the Sandman. We were dog tired and past prepared for a well-deserved slumber. We returned to the hotel. Later, Warren asked me how I felt.

I asked, "Why?"

He said, "Well you ate that thing with all the suckers!"

I responded, "Warren, I am from a city by the sea and eating fish is a part of that life."

He said, "Okay, if you're sure," and he went off to sleep.

We had made it. We were in Veracruz. That night as I entered the Halls of Moctezuma to accept my punishment, I wondered when my penance would finally be enough. Flushing the throne and praying for a calm and soothing night's sleep after surviving my first mutiny, I fell into bed and prayed for a solace of my soul. At first, a gentle peace filled my consciousness lowering my psyche into oblivion. But then, in an abrupt jerking motion of uncomfortable awareness of an intruder, there was my nemesis. The Grand Master of my misery, Moctezuma. This time he wore bright-blue macaw feathers, I guess for respect of the gulf's waters. He was chanting and dancing with a brutal looking Aztec war axe, displaying vicious obsidian blades that extended from the shaft. This was no plaything. He posed himself in an attack mode and waited for my one last request before the "coup de grace." What could I say, what could I do? Was there a point to all his abuse and innuendo? Hell if I knew. I just said, "Goodnight" and left him to his druthers. Maybe there was someone else he could share his antics with tonight. I couldn't care less. "Good night, sweet Prince."

18
SHARKS!
TUESDAY
JULY 1, 1975

It was all a bad dream, or was it? Did I spend half the night on my knees up-chucking octopus tentacles? Did my pounding head tell me anything in clarity of what happened in the last eight hours? What time was it anyway? Where was I? All this and more became clear when Warren and Tim entered the room and asked me how I was. Realizing I was weak as a kitten, it finally hit me, food poisoning. How old was that octopus anyway? Did they have to shave its beard before they served it to me? Oh crap, it was just bad luck, and now I had to live through it. But wait, I was on a field trip with eight people I was responsible for. With Warren and Tim staring at me in concern, I explained to them I had food poisoning.

The two of them looked at each other in agreement. "Octopus! We knew you shouldn't have eaten that!" they said.

Weakly, I responded, "There is nothing wrong with eating octopus, but the one I ate was old and spoiled."

"Sure!" they said, as they looked at each other all knowingly.

It was agreed they would let me rest and puke the rest of my guts out while they took the tribe and did a long walking tour of Veracruz and its harbor. They would return later and check on me to see if I was still alive, or if the octopus had taken me to the happy hunting grounds, or wherever they take difficult young white guys who think they know it all. What could I say, "Good luck." Then I got up suddenly and assumed the position in front of the toilet. "Welcome to Veracruz," I thought.

I don't remember any of it after that. I had sweated buckets, that I was sure of. My bed was soaked in fever sweat, but the headache was dissipating. Warren returned and checked on me. He could see I was recovering and would be okay. After breakfast, he had taken the whole crew throughout the city. After two days of nothing but riding in a cramped VW bus, everyone was happy to just be walking for a change. The added benefit of not having that bossy art teacher with them didn't hurt either. What a joy it must have been to critique his tutelage without his awareness or attendance. Who eats an octopus anyway? Crazy white bastard.

It was now afternoon, and I had somewhat recovered. The boys had suggested the idea of swimming. This sounded like a good idea since all I would have to do was sit in the water and possibly remark if someone was drowning. This was a good plan indeed. I gathered my physical reserves and met everyone down in the lobby. We loaded up in our faithful microbus and followed the waterfront south till it opened up to some public beach accesses. By this time, it was late afternoon. The light was a summer afterglow that reflected on the gulf surface and rippled in the incoming waves. It was beautiful. We parked on the beach, and the joyous multitude unloaded onto this welcoming scene. I was weak, but happy because they were happy. To observe a desert people take so freely to the salt waters of the Gulf of Mexico was quite visually amazing. Edgar White and Elvis Natan were natural swimmers. Who would have thunk?

As I soaked in the salt waters of the gulf, finally feeling the stress of my fever attack diminishing, I was grateful my tribe of Navajo warriors were able to allow me to convalesce that morning. Was it luck or good timing or were they really worried about me; I'll never know. Well, at least they didn't ditch me, grab the money and the keys, and run. Oh, that's right, I still had to sign checks for there to be more money. That was smart of American Express. You can't eliminate the guide if he is the bank. All right!

Everything was going swell. Seagulls were flying amongst us. Pelicans were dozing on docking posts keeping an eye on us. All was peaceful on God's green planet. As I drifted on my back on these highly salinized coastal waters, I heard a shout of inquiry coming from the boys. "Shows, is that a shark fin?"

My lackadaisical, restive consciousness awakened to that one noun in the English language that demands a response anywhere near water, "Shark?" I asked.

Edgar and Elvis were pointing to vertical fins not six feet away from them, three of them. These desert boys had never seen sharks before, otherwise they most certainly would have hustled back to the beach. I shouted for them to return immediately and got everybody out of the water right then. I think the thing that saved us was there were nine bodies moving in the water at one time, and the sharks couldn't decide on a victim. Whatever, we all got to the beach safely and watched as those fins cruised the waters we had recently exited, looking for afternoon appetizers. Only then did Warren point out to me a sign that said, *Peligro! Tiburones!* (Danger, Sharks!)

"Why didn't you say something? "I said.

"I didn't see the sign until we got out," he said. Oh well, we were alive, and all body parts were accounted for.

We made it back to the hotel and got dressed. The sun had set, and we were ready for dinner after a long afternoon of swimming. We had *hamburguesas* (hamburgers) and *papas fritas* (French fries) that night, what else? While in the water, Warren and I had planned the next leg of our journey. If we doubled back to Doblado, we could connect to Route

150, and this road would give us a straight shot to Puebla. Letting the boys know we would be leaving the next morning, we knew after the active day they had had walking the historic city and swimming with sharks all afternoon, they were inevitably ready for a good night's rest.

My sheets had been changed, God bless the staff, and since there was nothing in my body until just recently, I knew a great night's rest was finally on my dance card. I couldn't wait. Thanking Tim and Warren for getting me through that day, we then all dropped to our beds and wandered into dreamland. Ah, oblivion, the greatest gift of all. "Hello, come on, really!" Moctezuma stood there leering at me with another one of those damn snakes in his teeth. Talk about disgusting, he stared in his most ferocious grimace and grunted loudly as he approached me. What could I say, what could I do? So, in terrified acknowledgement I said, "Your majesty, eat me. I'm too tired for this."

19
PUEBLA
WEDNESDAY
JULY 2, 1975

Our tribe, feeling refreshed and recharged after a day of exercise and with full stomachs, was hesitantly prepared for the next leg of our trip. Though, at this time, they had all accepted going home was a good idea. There was also the dim reality of what we were going home to—reservation life. Essentially, there was nothing wrong with that. This was the ending of an adventure that would be missing from that equation. The truth was, our journey had not been uneventful, thanks to Chee and Leon, and there still was a chance of seeing us behind bars. There was just no telling what the future still held in reserve for this unprepared troop of wanderers into these mysterious lands of Aztlán.

After breakfast, the whole crew packed the microbus with suitcases, and a few students even added small bags of seashells the sharks had been willing to part with. Well, at least we had these shells to prove we made it to the Gulf of Mexico since we had no receipts or treasures to prove any of our other adventures.

After everyone was situated in their usual seat and ready to go, someone shouted one last dig at me as I started the van, "Hey, Shows, you gonna miss that octopus?"

Ha ha, very funny I thought, and we were off. Puebla, here we come.

The road was all uphill once we passed Orizaba. Route 150 took us through the cities of Nogales and Los Reyes de Juarez, also along the way. We had been able to view Pico de Orizaba, which stood at 18,406 feet, the highest point in all of Mexico. This wondrous volcano was again nature's way of reminding us of what bothersome members of creation we were, and we nine took the lesson to heart. The landscapes, if you could call the magnificent tracts of vista that were obviously some of the most treasured and richly endowed of nature's beneficence, were breathtaking. It was obvious to us; this was *rico* (rich) country, and we were intruders. The beauty of our ascension on the up-road climb to Puebla was extraordinary. This experience was a gift for all our struggles through the lower jungles of the country. The air was fresh. The humid oppression of the sea level altitudes disappeared as we rose into the higher stratosphere of the upper plateau onto Puebla. We were reinvigorated by this altitude's blessed coolness and responded with a refreshed attitude of optimism. The boys were showing signs of recovery, and that was good.

I'd been keeping an attentive eye on Leon and Chee. I could see they were getting restless and that could only mean one thing. Trouble was coming. Well, until it manifested, there wasn't much I could do except wait for the earth to move and be prepared to dance around the pitfalls of their connivances. I was on my own when it came to those two. No one else was going to lend support to this *Bellagaana* (white person) teacher who was not a member of their tribe. He was on his own.

Entering Puebla was beyond indescribable. Maybe it was the fresh exhilaration of the mountain air we had missed since our dear home New Mexico, or we simply were ready to attend to the one final destination. Whatever the reason, Puebla was a well-needed therapeutic band aid at this time for the heart and soul. The city itself was encompassed in a valley between four volcanoes. Within the basin of these natural boundaries, a thriving, prosperous, and most extraordinary cultural example of traditional Mexico shone. We, as a group, were enthused at its possibilities through the windshield of our magic bus.

Route 150 brought us directly to the city square. Making a left on Heroes del Cinco de Mayo, we drove to the intersection of Avenue de la Reforma and turned right. Driving slowly through this main historic section of the center of Pueblo, we passed the Church of Campana, then the House of Dolls, and finally came to the Palacio Municipal on the central *plaza* (square) of the city. From here, we began our search for a hotel suggested on our rental car map. The *plaza* (square) was bustling; there was activity everywhere. There were jugglers, musicians, magicians, and all in colorful outfits. The city was a kaleidoscope of color in itself.

With incredible luck, we found our hotel, and with even more incredible luck, they had three rooms. It seems Wednesday was being kind to us. Parking our van in a tiny guest parking lot, we dispersed from the bus and filed into a small, but in some ways spacious, operation. The hotel was well attended by a staff who obviously cared for this sweet old building, occupying a key location in the historic district. Though the rooms were small and tight, they were the cleanest and most pleasant in all our travels so far. This would be our last hotel in Mexico. Tomorrow we would be in Mexico City, and there we would catch the night train home. This was indeed our last night in a city of beauty and charm to remember for the rest of our lives. Well, at least I acknowledged that fact, the boys had other priorities. Still, I could tell they were impressed with what they saw.

We left the hotel for the *plaza* (square). Here, as I stated, was a menagerie of visual and auditory stimulus. There was a theatrical performance that I eventually recognized as acts from "The Man of la Mancha" by Cervantes. Puebla was obviously not only the historical salvation of Mexico over the French, but it was also an academically cultural foundation to Mexico in general. There was pride in this city, not just of Puebla, but a kind of beating heart to this whole nation of heroes. These people, of a multitude of individual cultures, were contributing to a greater one by the name of Mexico, *Viva* (Long live) Mexico!

My tribe and I walked and gawked and gasped at entertainers and performers, and this was a Wednesday. Soon we found ourselves at the city market. Here we discovered the magnificent burnished black pottery of the Indios unique to Puebla. For a *centavo* (cent) of a moment, just a moment, I could imagine pulling up the microbus and loading it with as much of this black gold as I could manage and driving it to the US to make my fortune. This is how much I was taken by the crafts of Mexico. The work we were seeing in this city far surpassed any we had observed elsewhere in the country. There was just a quality and pride apparent in everything we saw.

After viewing the Regional Museum of Puebla, our human fuel gauge was starting to lean towards empty. But it wasn't just food we needed; it was time to go home. We were finally showing "travel drag" as a result of our ambitious odyssey into Aztlán. Our fair New Mexico was calling, and we were finally listening. At dinner, Warren and I went over the next day's plans and schedules and imparted that info to the group. After a splendid meal only a city like this could provide, we trailed off to our hotel and to our last bed rest of our trip. Tomorrow it was Mexico City.

I won't lie to you. The curse was alive and well and residing quite happily in my body of standing pain. I don't mention my constant awareness of it because who would really want to know? Suffice it to say, the emperor was holding me prisoner, and I was at his beck and call. After another episode of our arrangement in his throne room, I made it to bed. Again, Tim and Warren were off to dreamland, probably dancing with beautiful Navajo girls or *senoritas* (young women) and enjoying themselves mightily. Soon I faded into a slumber and thought--- at last a quiet night. Maybe I have escaped the wrath of his visit finally, maybe?

Then some humming began. Was that hissing? There he was, again covered in gold and feathers like the first time I saw him. He held two snakes pointed at me, why? What was their significance? We were leaving on the night train tomorrow. We would be leaving Moctezuma's empire soon, he should be happy, at least to be rid of my white European ass. He continued to press the two great rattlesnakes towards me, insistently. Wait a minute, the last time he pulled the snake thing was when Chee and Leon had been up to their shenanigans. Was this a warning of impending disaster concerning the daring duo? Was Moctezuma more afraid of those two than of me, ha? I guess even a fierce, old Aztec emperor is reluctant to take on two wily, Native high school boys up to no good. Thinking this out loud, I laughed and said to my captor, "And you thought Cortez was trouble. Try being a high school teacher sometime." And at that, sleep took me by the hand and led me away.

Volcano at Puebla

20
THE LONG
AND WINDING ROAD
THURSDAY
JULY 3, 1975

While packing to leave, I grabbed my last clean shirt from the bottom of my bag, and lo and behold, there were three rolls of used slide film sitting at the bottom. So, there would be something to prove we had been in Mexico and not Las Vegas, Nevada. Well now, this puts a whole new spin on the results of our trip. I wondered what was on the photo shots of those rolls, Teotihuacan and the pyramid of the sun and moon possibly? They had obviously been taken from early in the trip. Even so, I wouldn't know until we returned home and had them developed. It was at least something. There was now hope that I could still pull this off as a legitimate school field trip with photo documentation to prove it. Thank you, Jesus.

We loaded up the magic bus and bid adieu to our wonderful stay in Puebla. I still thought about those beautiful burnished black Indio pots, and how if I didn't have a busload of kids, I could fill the VW with them from front to back and head for the border, oh well. As we were ascending toward the western volcano of Puebla, I noticed something that my memory had tucked away and was suddenly retrieving. This magnificently posed, snowcapped mountain trailed by us and presented a sloped valley, which ran the entire length of the vista and helped me pinpoint that image in my brain, but there was one difference. There had been no snow on the volcano cap in that reference, instead it had been smoking, and in the valley marched conquistadors and their camp followers towards Moctezuma's Aztec Mexican empire. This was not any kind of foresight, it was the memory of Tyrone Power in the "Captain of Castillo," filmed in 1947. At the time, quite an accomplishment for Hollywood and the Mexican government. The film had obviously affected me in my youth, enough that I saw exactly where that last movie scene had been shot and marveled at how impactful that image was to have crawled into my lizard brain and been trapped there. It appears the mind is a fabulous reservoir of flowing memories, one need only dip into every once in a while, to refresh the soul.

From this wondrous peak, the roller coaster ride down to Mexico City began. We followed Route 150 and would integrate into 190 to flow seamlessly into eastern Mexico City. It was about this time I caught my nemesis, my Mr. Christian, through the rearview mirror plotting with the crew. Seeing me, he pretended to look innocent, but Chee was clearly spouting some Navajo in a convincing harangue of arguments all were listening to. What diabolical plan had he hashed up last night in his sleep? As we were nearing the outskirts of Mexico City, his planned attack began. First, stealthily, with comments about how the boys had suffered so to endure this merciless journey into this foreign land, there were insinuations of some needful recompense due them. Then, there began a general grumbling of how restrictive and controlling the *Belagaana* (white person) teacher in charge was, AKA, me. And finally, to the central point of the grievance, a demand for a party with booze to celebrate their survival under such abject conditions placed on their lives following the previous duration.

Ah! Now I understood his well-thought-out strategy. Until now, every one of Chee's misdeeds was on a personal nature, but finally he had contrived a plan that would work with the support of the group as a whole. Thank God, he had been too selfish to come up with this approach earlier, otherwise, I might have ended up stuck in the middle of the Isthmus talking to a five-inch-long cockroach while Chee, Leon, and the whole crew drove away without me. This was a fortuitous fact, timing wise, but I still had to get this ship of fools home safely. What to do, what to do? They continued grumbling, and the plan of taking over the ship seemed eminent. I looked at Warren, no help there. I looked at Tim, his expression made it apparent, "Don't look at me!" So, I was screwed. How do I get eight Navajos home safely without getting burned at the stake in the process?

If I got caught buying the boys alcohol, I would lose my job. If I allowed them to buy alcohol on their own, I was also screwed. If I let Warren buy them alcohol, I was an accessory to the fact. There was no way out for me, either I came up with some solution fast, or I would be rowing a lifeboat on my own back to merry old England, AKA, Captain Blye. Let's be honest, the only thing that couldn't be forgiven would be not getting my charges home alive. So, being trapped between a rock and an empty bottle, I made a proposal, "If all of you promise to behave yourselves all the way back to El Paso, and I mean no trouble, we will have a party there before we go home." Chee had won, But I still held the cards and had played what I had been dealt. I felt I was still in the game.

Entering the city in late morning, I drove us to the train station first, to check the night schedule. There was a departure at six o'clock. Next, we drove to the rental car agency to turn in our faithful magic bus. On the way there we again saw the plexiglass cubes covering ancient, recently excavated, treasures that subway construction had raised from the dead. It was hard to believe all these recovered artifacts had been hidden since Hernan Cortez's conquest. The reality of subway construction was recovering the cultural foundation of this great nation and showing the world the magnificence of its Indigenous heritage. At the moment though, none of this would be apparent, but as time presented the opportunity of this nation to realize the potential of the commercial aspect of tourism on a whole, the bounty of this recovery would be unquestionable.

Getting closer to our destination we hit a stoplight and while waiting, I happened to see a black woman standing outside a hotel alone in some sort of quandary. Since I was waiting at this long light, I shouted over, "Are You having problems?"

Seeing me and shocked to hear any English spoken, she responded, "Yes, I can't get a cab. I don't speak Spanish."

I told her I would pull over and help her and was able to cut the corner and hugging the curb, I stopped and then asked her where she needed to go. In the meantime my tribe, most who had never seen a black person before, were wondering what a white guy was doing trying to help a black woman.

When the woman neared the van, she viewed the whole crew and me, and you could see from the whites of her eyes she wasn't sure if this was a war party or not and in Mexico City, huh? I explained to her this was a teaching field trip from New Mexico, and we were preparing to go home today. She calmed down, told me where she needed to go, and I offered her a ride there since I just happened to know, through experience with the city map, where it was. Hesitantly, she got in, the Eriacho brothers made enough room for her to fit, and we were off. On the way to her destination, probably due to nerves, this nice woman filled us in on her purpose in Mexico City. Turns out, 1975 was The United Nation's World Women's Conference, and it was being held in Mexico City. She was the representative from Detroit and had no idea what she had gotten herself into, but she was here and trying to make the best of it.

She was still staring at all of us in the bus, I'm sure wondering when we would tie her up and take her to our campsite and have our way with her, but we were on a tight schedule and only had time to drop her off at the conference center in the historic district. We wished her luck, and driving away I wondered how she would explain that a band of American Indians got her to her conference on time. Oh well, life is just a sequence of unexpected stories.

We rediscovered our old car rental agency and pulled in. After observing us with all our weariness so apparent, the dealership made things painless and easy. In time we were square and after gathering our luggage, we marched off to search for a decent lunch. After hiking a series of endless blocks, we found a cafe outside what turned out to be a municipal crafts market. So, after consuming our native vitals, we went shopping. As you recall, I had promised the boys a last market day due to the "Grand Theft" we experienced in Villahermosa. This situation fit our time and location imperative, so Warren and I strolled through the market with the boys, helping them negotiate for either new or replacement prizes they had lost previously. They were happy. Warren and I were glad to reciprocate any goodwill, knowing the long train ride home was going to wipe them out.

When the shopping was complete and smiles were covering all the boys faces, we started looking for taxis. Up until now, there were taxis glutting the street outside the market, but by the time we finished shopping, it was rush hour. It was now five o'clock. Oh shit! Warren, Tim and I started waving down any stray taxi that wasn't occupied and with no luck. We were in trouble; our train was leaving in one hour. And then somehow, Tim snagged us a taxi, and I was lucky to grab another one. The drivers asked us where our destination was, and we told them the train station. It was at this point I realized they were starting to appear in the visage of the infamous Pancho Villa. While twirling their mustaches, I became aware these banditos were quite cognizant of the train schedules and intended on holding us up mercilessly. After surrendering to their terms, which basically ransomed our souls, we took off at warp speed to the central train station and somehow made it in enough time to get our tickets and load onto a moving train. The clammer of our baggage, loading into the overhead racks of the train car, did cause a disturbance, and soon a conductor appeared and was about to challenge us, until he saw who we were, and remembering us from three weeks previous, he skedaddled away as quickly as his little feet would carry him. For some mysterious reason we did not encounter him the remainder of the train trip. We had made it, thanks to small miracles along the way. As the train pulled out of the railyard and started passing the old wooden revolutionary train cars, we started to recover our composure and be aware that this was it. We were leaving. We were going home.

Mexico City and all that we had seen and experienced throughout this country would soon be the stuff of dreams and memories laying low in our exhausted consciousness. I didn't know about the boys, but I knew it would take me decades to explore the bank of my memories to even come close to recalling all that we had experienced and endured. For now, we were headed north, and I was getting my crew, tenuously, back to the US. This adventure was not over though, not by a long shot.

21
THE CALM BEFORE THE STORM
FRIDAY
JULY 4, 1975

There is not much to write about a train ride rattling down the tracks toward home. The first night was spent in a stupor of exhaustion, relief, regret, and questions. Had we really been too tired to continue our adventure east to Chetumal? Were we simply too afraid the dynamic duo would eventually get us arrested and locked away in some jungle prison? Then also, had we missed the most monumental aspects of a more persistent delving into the wonders of Aztlán? Were there still hidden mysteries abounding in locations we could have explored but failed in our quest? Well, of course, but like all actual explorers, there were limits as to the possibilities available on each individual adventure.

The unknown elements of an intended journey are of course the reward at its end. And it is not what you didn't accomplish at the end, but what you did, and if you returned home alive to tell the story. That, in itself, is all that matters, right? This all sounds like a most credible bit of reasoning, but no matter who you are, there is always a lingering regret not to have gone further, to have seen more, done more. It is simply human nature never to be satisfied. There is always more. Right?

As we wound through the train stops on our trek home, we visually followed the changing terrain through the train car's windows. Slowly we would be coming upon the Chihuahuan desert, and that desert essentially led all the way to Santa Fe, New Mexico itself, home sweet home. Still, recent memories of our journey were fresh in our minds. I knew there was much my students would never absorb of this complex country south of our home state. Yet there was much to consider in the cultural immersion they had participated in. What was a Mexican, what was an Indio? Who is an American, what is an Indian? Who are we, period? These students had a whole new cosmology to now consider. Whether they would ever even waste the time to review these philosophical points in question made no difference. The fact that they had been part of an extensive cultural odyssey, the things they saw, the people they met, whether these individuals sold them sodas, or cleaned their hotel rooms, they were all part of this unique experience that would lay in wait in their memories for their own future storytelling to future generations.

As for myself, I had begun dreaming in Spanish. I had often heard you really know you are picking up a language when you start dreaming in it. So, for my active brain's current memory, I was still somehow in Mexico, at least as far as my subconscious was concerned. It would be months for this to pass, but I was impressed at how the brain adapted to this function of linguistic survival. Funny, huh?

We ate when the vendors came through at the train stops. We slept in between those stops. The rest you get on a train is not a stationary rest. So, there really is no sleep per se, it is more like a constant snoozing as your body gently shifts with every breaking in the tracks, clickety-clack, clickety-clack. Our minds tumbled throughout the day and night with conscious and unconscious images in somewhat a dream state. Our bodies were going home, but how long would it take our minds to catch up? Time would only tell, but in the meantime the train continued to chug and chug north to our own land of *manana* (tomorrow). We were, like it or not, homeward bound.

22
EL PASO, GATEWAY TO THE UNITED STATES
SATURDAY
JULY 5, 1975

Rattling through the second night across lonely, moon-lit, desert vistas, we eventually saw the early light of dawn, and by midmorning, the outskirts of Juarez started to appear. This ride from Mexico City was particularly grueling after all our adventures compounded. We were just dog-tired and weary.

Pulling into our final destination, the train yard of Juarez, we gradually regained consciousness and started addressing reality by gradually collecting our things. The Eriacho brothers, Orlando and Cooper, of course, had new guitars they had purchased at the market before we left. The other boys had repurchased other things including, of course, Mexican cowboy hats. These purchases had helped heal some of the disappointment created by the great "Villahermosa" theft. As a result, there was much more than their bags to haul when you counted in their loot. We would most definitely need taxis. With everything piled up on the curb, Tim and I hunted for them. Without much trouble, we found two old drivers willing to take us to the border. I truly don't even know if they were legal taxis, but hell, it was Juarez. You took what you got.

The ride was so rough, our teeth rattled all the way to the border bridge to the US. The fact that I could see the road through openings in the floor of the vehicle barely aroused my consciousness to the danger. Someone would eventually fall through but hopefully not today.

We arrived at the bridge, and carrying our loot, marched to the US immigration entrance. There were no passports required back then, all we had were our Mexican visas and Warren and I had our New Mexico driver's licenses. So, after asking what a tall, white guy with eight Navajos were doing in Mexico, the US immigration agent smiled unbelievably at the ridiculous statement behind our school field trip adventure. We were too tired to make any effort to convince him beyond a doubt, and I suppose because he could see our apparent exhaustion, decided it wasn't worth questioning us further and released us to continue to our home country, The United States of America.

We found our way to a small cafe not far from the border bridge. Here we piled up our belongings and ordered breakfast. God, we were tired. I don't know how many breakfasts we had, it had been so long since we had eaten, and plain American food just hit the spot. Slowly recovering, thanks to the nutrients coursing through our bodies, and being finally released from the clickety clacking of the train tracks vibrating through our bodies, we slowly became aware we were home, well at least in the US that is. This was Texas, and we New Mexicans were always leery of Texas.

Any who, having recovered somewhat, I asked the waitress of the cafe if there were any hotels nearby that we could walk to. She, a pleasant lady, directed us some blocks to a Holiday Inn which happened to be right near the Greyhound bus station, Eureka! Leaving an exaggerated tip, to thank her for all her help and her assistance to a band of marauding Indians and that token white guy, we strolled off with a bit more energy than when we had arrived. The day was a border town, sun scorched, burning sidewalk, invitation to hell. Well, to say the least, it was hot. We made it to the Holiday Inn and thanks to no early check-in requirements yet, we appropriated our three rooms. Of course, there were no problems checking in early, who in their right mind would even be in El Paso in July, unless they had to be there.

Dragging all our stuff noisily to our rooms, we started occupying our final digs. Everyone, without stating the obvious, just fell onto the beds, and in the cool air conditioning, the first of the entire trip, passed out into sleep. Tim Maria, Warren, and I followed suit and collapsed heavily from our personal fatigues. Except for the sound of air conditioning, all was quiet. Lying there peaceful and immobile, I said a prayer of thanks for getting us home alive. No one had lost a limb. No one had died, and no one was incarcerated and left behind in a prison or jail in Mexico. All in all, luck had blessed our trip and returned us to our home sweet home. For all the calamities accumulated along the way, I had brought my tribe back alive. There was much to be proud of. Wait when they hear the stories back home. Yes, sirree, I was a hero, there was no questioning that fact.

Bang, Bang, Bang, suddenly, there was pounding on the door of our room. What the hell. Pulling myself back to this world, I awoke and went to answer the door. Come on, I thought to myself, I paid with travelers' checks, there shouldn't be any problems.

Opening the door with an unnecessary aggressive jerk, there stood Chee Dodge Martine and Leon Martin, and the words from their mouths haunt me even to this very day, "What about our party?"

It was now one o'clock. Looking at my two nemeses, my two mutineers, I had to think quickly. "It's too early for a party. You'll have to wait until sundown." This was not taken well.

The two looked at me cross eyed and waited for more.

"Okay, at four o'clock you can have a party, but not until then. I'll get refreshments and drinks and you be back at our room at that time," I said.

Still not pleased, but somewhat placated, the two collaborators to my future dismissal as an educator left, and now the clock was ticking.

In a while, Warren awoke, and I discussed our predicament now that the boys had recovered enough to remember the party promise. Together we planned an event with hopefully the least amount of alcoholic influence possible, and yet, hopefully, would soothe the appetite of this youthful war band. About three o'clock we strolled on down the scorching El Paso sidewalk to look for the needed supplies that would fulfill our designs of this so-called party. On the way though, we ran into the Greyhound bus station and checked early morning schedules for Albuquerque, New Mexico. Luck was with us, there was a Sunday morning seven o'clock bus to our destination, home. This was good news. We wouldn't realize until Sunday though, how good this news really was.

Returning to our search for supplies for a party for high school boys that would most certainly terminate our employment future as teachers, we stumbled upon a delinquent looking liquor store with some meager offerings of snacks on the shelves as well as dusty old liquor bottles searching for desperate buyers. After surveying the limited premises, we decided on purchasing a case of Budweiser, a six pack of coke, three large bags of tostados, and two bags of pretzels. We found a couple of cans of bean dip, compliments of Frito Lay, to top off this feast. Also grabbing some snacks for Tim Maria, Warren, and me, we hauled our banquet back up the city sidewalks to the Holiday Inn and waited in our room for the witching hour of four o'clock. Warren and I looked at each other one last time as part of the Ramah Navajo teaching staff. We were absolutely convinced, once we got back and word got out that we had allowed these students a party with booze, our careers would be dust in the wind. Of this we had no doubts.

As if they were standing by the door of our room with a stopwatch, there was a very hard knocking at exactly four o'clock sharp. There they were, all of them, six weary, sharp-eyed boys, intent on the celebration of a lifetime held in a Holiday Inn in beautiful downtown El Paso, Texas. Who could ask for anything more?

We gave them everything but the six pack of coke and a bag of pretzels. We were not partaking of the beer, that much we had agreed upon. Our past experience had forewarned us of that mistake. We would sit in our room, watch TV, and wait for the fireworks. We knew Chee wouldn't let us down.

During this time, I also made a call to the school hoping someone might be working overtime since we were all preparing to move to our newly constructed modern school complex duly named Pine Hill for its setting.

As luck would have it, Jim Wolfe, an ex-Catholic priest, now married and working as one of our administrators, answered the phone, "Hello," said he.

"Oh, thank God you're there, Jim, we just got back from Mexico. We're in El Paso and are going to be in Albuquerque tomorrow afternoon. Could Herbert Henio pick us up?" I asked.

Jim hesitated somewhat on the line, and then he said that tomorrow was Sunday, and Herbert couldn't pick us up till Monday, sorry.

I thanked Jim and hung up. What could I do? We would have to spend a day in Albuquerque it seemed. Well heck, that was that.

Tim, Warren and I watched some program or other on the television, nothing spectacular. I think we were just happy to hear English spoken to us from a glass picture tube. We hadn't heard the language outside ourselves for three weeks. It was kind of novel. I'd forgotten once you leave your home country that time stops as far as news and current events. It's like you're a space traveler, and you finally land on your home planet and discover time has forgotten all about you and moved on with life without you, funny huh?

At five-fifteen there was a pounding on our door. One hour and fifteen minutes had passed, that's all. Looking at the faces of Warren and Tim, I knew I was all alone. I was the sacrificial lamb, "Nice knowing ya." Opening the door on the third eruption of fist blows, Chee had them all lined up in front of him, but he, of course, was to be their spokesman.

A case of Budweiser beer, divided amongst six individuals, is not a lot of alcohol. But young adolescent bodies were going to be a lot more susceptible to its influence than adults. As they stared at me in befuddled arrogant anticipation, I asked them, "What's up?"

They then stared in perplexed confusion until Chee Dodge piped up, "Shows, we want more beer, you didn't buy us enough, you promised us a party. Go get some more!"

This is one of those points in your little life that you really never expected nor ever thought you deserved, but there it is. I told them, "I promised you a party, and I delivered. You're all drunk, and that was enough booze. Why don't you go back to your rooms and watch television. Tomorrow, we catch the bus to Albuquerque."

From the looks on their faces, I don't think my idea was going to sink in anywhere. They were on the warpath and needed results, not recreational suggestions for a quiet evening. A calamitous, vicious eruption of vocal shouts and outrageous threats ensued. These boys were hot, and nothing was going to cool their ardor. I was going down. Goodbye, sweet world.

Chee Dodge finally moved to the front of the crowd with Leon and was shouting the loudest, "You promised us a party!"

By this time, worried the hotel might throw us all out, I tried to calm this lynch mob. I only had seconds to resolve the situation before there was no hope of a solution. The clock was ticking. There are no verbal resolutions when dealing with a drunken mob. I had no six guns, no badge, no hope of coming out of this alive. I was both the sheriff and the prisoner, and I was going to hang high.

The emotional trap I had placed myself in was complete. I was their prisoner, so I did what any prisoner would do in this situation, I started bawling like a baby, sobbing in front of them. In a moment, I told them I was disappointed with them. "Together, we had explored the country of Mexico and seen wonders of an ancient world many people only dream about. We had escaped the police, no thanks to Chee and Leon, and also sharks in Veracruz. No throats had been cut by barbers in Merida, and all treasures lost in Villahermosa had been replaced or improved upon thanks to the market in Mexico City." Sobbing all the way through my dissertation, I finally burst out in a screaming wretch, "And I brought you back alive as well. After all that, you want to jump me and beat me up?"

Except for my sobs, there was complete silence. How do you beat up a six-foot three pussy who cries? This was embarrassing them. What to do, what to do? They gathered themselves together, and after witnessing such a disgusting display of pathetic emotion, they turned around and returned from whence they came, embarrassed for me and themselves for having to have witnessed this display.

Once they were gone, I turned around and saw Tim and Warren staring at me in shock. "Well, what was I supposed to do, duke it out? It was all that I could come up with." They stared at me mystified. At this point, I grabbed for the old rotary phone in the room and tried the school number one last time for the hell of it. I was at the end of my rope, out of gas, kaput. Yet again, another miracle occurred. Jim Wolf was just leaving the office but grabbed the phone one last time as it rang. "Jim, don't hang up. I can't wait till Monday with this crew. We have been through too much, and we are all at our wits' end. If Herbert can't pick us up tomorrow in Albuquerque, I'm walking away and leaving the group in your hands. You can be responsible for their safety." There was a silence, a few seconds of suspense one has to breathe through.

Finally, Jim said, "Let me get a hold of Herbert and see what can be done. What time do you arrive in Albuquerque?"

I filled him in on the details of our schedule and hung up. We sat and waited for what seemed an hour, and the phone rang eventually.

"Andy, Herbert will be there to pick you up and bring you home," he said.

In response, I thanked Jim, told him I was sorry for the dramatics and just reiterated our exhaustive journey had rung us out. As a crew we were simply out of gas to boot. There were no more metaphors necessary, he understood. I wished him a good night and hung up.

The rest of the evening was spent watching TV, and from the corner of my eye, watching Tim and Warren watching me. I could see they still hadn't decided if I was a superb actor or an embarrassing crybaby at heart. Why can't you be both? Later we hit the sack. Using the throne room one last time before sleep, it occurred to me His Majesty, Emperor Moctezuma, had been delinquent of his duties. Was that it? Was I free of his punishment? Had crossing the border cured me? Had it all been travel stress? What the heck, who knew? I lay in my bed marveling at my two escapes from death, one from the emperor, one from my student hordes. Tomorrow we would be home, the long journey completed, and it would take some time to see if I still had a job. How would this drunken episode play out in the real world? I didn't know, but I knew I was dead tired, and I finally surrendered to the guards in my sleep cell.

23
THE FINAL STRAW
SUNDAY
JULY 6, 1975

Sunday morning in El Paso, Texas, you just can't find enough words to describe the place. Because it was booted up next to New Mexico, Texas barely acknowledged the place as one of its own cities. What they had done though, was plant pollution spewing factories on the Mexican side of the border, so they wouldn't be responsible to the EPA for the filth they produced. In the meantime, the real money lived in El Paso proper and spent all their days counting their ill-gotten gains. In short, nothing has changed in this town since Pancho Villa bought guns and military stores from the ancestors of these same families. Business was business on the border. Outside of that, El Paso was just another border town itself. These were not the birth places of the American Dream, instead they were a warning of the hopelessness created by a local blood-sucking white economy who engaged in a mercenary approach to immigration. This was a socially imposed purgatory through an entrapment of financial exploitation. In short, in 1975, El Paso sucked.

We got the boys up early. Some were experiencing their first hangover. Well, they couldn't have been that bad considering how little they had consumed. We grabbed snacks in the bus station, and then we sat on old benches, being careful to avoid some puke left from a previous visitor, yuck! At seven o'clock, we purchased our one-way tickets to good old Albuquerque, New Mexico. It didn't look like there were many riders outside of us, so we'd be able to stretch out in the seats and snooze off. Our luggage and treasures were collected onto a bus company cart and hauled off for loading on our particular Greyhound transport. Everything felt copacetic, and the previous evening's antics were now in the past. We were a wandering tribe of teacher and students again, and we were going home.

The bus station in El Paso was a loose-run operation. Everything felt slipshod and intentionally relaxed. I became extremely cautious of everything I was witnessing. As we were finally loading, I told Tim Maria, who was at the end of the bus, to keep an eye on our baggage cart and make sure they loaded all our stuff. We then climbed up like the Sunday morning stragglers we were, finding double seats for all of us. The driver showed up, he took one look at us, and jumped in his seat and started the bus. He probably wouldn't take another look until he got to Albuquerque. Backing out of the station, I finally remembered the job I had given Tim, "Hey Tim, did they load our bags?"

Tim rallied himself, took a look and suddenly shouted, "Hell no, the cart is still sitting right there in the bus yard."

At that, I shouted to the driver, "Stop!" He gave me an indignant look, but I marched up to him, pointed out our belongings sitting behind us in the lot, then he finally accepted our objections. Backing up, we found the baggage guy, hungover, and prodded him into loading our things. Now we could leave.

I'm sure none of us remember the drive between El Paso and Albuquerque. The beginning of the real travel weariness, which had accumulated over the past three weeks in Mexico, and which would take us probably another three weeks to acclimate—physically, psychologically, and emotionally, finally set upon us. No one was aware we were even at our destination until the driver piped up, "Albuquerque, New Mexico!" Our blurry eyes blinked open, and we slowly became aware of where we were. It was late afternoon when we arrived and unloaded. The stops along the way, including Las Cruces, Socorro, Belen, and Los Lunas, had dragged this route out to a long-extended journey, but I doubt anyone was even awake to notice.

Gathering our things from the bus's baggage compartment below, we slowly marched out to the street in front of the Greyhound bus station in downtown Albuquerque. This, at the time, was a particularly bleak part of the inner city of Albuquerque's downtown. Eventually, this bus station would be demolished, and I believe the new police central headquarters was built in its place. Our luck it seems was still with us, and good old Herbert Henio was standing outside with the school van waiting for us. Thank you, Jesus. We slowly moved like condemned men from an ordeal of an unmistakably challenging duration of prison time. We were beat, but we were finally almost home.

These last two hours of riding were quiet. It appeared everyone was wrapped within his own introspection. Even Chee Dodge just stared out the window. Were we glad to be home? Were we not glad to be home? Travel exhaustion seemed to have simply wiped our consciousness clean of any clear evaluation for the moment. Only time would eventually put the experience into perspective. Still, there's no place like home. As we trekked down Route 53, the route of the ancient Anasazi, Coronado, The United States Camel Cavalry, and countless other travelers and explorers, we observed Bandera Crater's peak and knew we were nearing our destination. Huge ponderosas lined the road and raised their limbs to welcome us home and appeared to cheer us on to the finish line. We were almost there.

El Morro National Monument stood proudly in the Sunday afternoon sunlight to remind us of where we were. Each turn in the road brought us closer to the end of our adventure, and mile by mile we were able to recognize home again. Dropping down the last hill we gently curved into the village of Ramah past the post office and the Lewis Trading Post and eventually into the parking lot of our old school.

We stopped in front of the school office buildings, really, just a collection of trailers, old prefab buildings and an hogan that no one even knew the origin of how it had even gotten there to begin with. What was surprising was on a Sunday afternoon there were a number of people around. I supposed they were packing for the transfer to the new school complex. Otherwise, why would they be there?

It was then I noticed members of the Literary Society, our poker club, standing about and watching as we parked. There was Larry, the school director, Marshall and Gilbert, both administrative officers, and even our principle. They were just standing around with curious expressions on their faces. Now somehow, in a fraction of a second, I caught pocket movement on two of them and glimpsed green cash being passed over to another. I'll probably never know who bet on what, but what ta' hell! I wondered what the odds were.

It was strange that everyone else came out of the buildings when we arrived. They stood outside in the late afternoon heat lined up, and for one glorious moment, I swear, I thought they were going to salute me. But they didn't. Still the feeling of amazement at our survival and eventual return must have kept the daily boredom of school office work at bay for some. We were hero travelers whose legendary exploits would roll off the tongues of high school students for centuries to come. Oh hell, I think our audience was really just glad we got home in one piece.

Warren and I got out of the bus. Herbert would drop the boys off at their homes on the reservation on the way to his. I took one last look at my traveling tribe. There was Edgar White, Elvis Natan, the Eriacho brothers, Cooper and Orlando, and of course, there was Chee Dodge, and Leon Martin. I gave a wink to Tim Maria. I would certainly owe him for the rest of my life. This group of Argonauts had survived ancient Aztlán and returned to tell the story.

They looked at me with blurry eyes and incomprehensive stares. Maybe in a few days they'd come to and wonder what the heck they've done the last three weeks and then piece it together, or not. Who knows, they were high school kids. I waved goodbye, told them I'd see them when school began, I hoped, and stood there as Herbert pulled away throwing dust from the wheels in my face.

Warren Roanhorse was standing near me and was about to say goodbye. At the last second, I asked him, "Warren, if you have time, would you write from your memory, an outline of our past itinerary of our travels, day-to-day. Something I could use for the school assembly."

He said, "Sure, I'll get it to you later."

I didn't know if I would ever get it, but at least the sentiment was there.

Walking home from the school was not far for me. My roommate, Ron, and I rented an old Mormon farmhouse bowed on a rock pinnacle and built of ammo boxes from World War II, home sweet home. Dragging myself up the rugged drive to the house took the last few ounces of strength I had. I don't even remember opening the door. I stripped down for bed and visited the "Hole of Calcutta" one last time before I retired to my rest. I felt an overwhelming exhaustion cleansing my soul, well not really, maybe just a purging of three weeks of anxiety, whatever.

I was home, in my own bed, preparing to sleep the sleep of heroes. I had brought everyone back alive, "Yippee!" Now go to sleep, you ego indulgent poor excuse for a human, RIP.

Dozing off rapidly, I suddenly remembered Moctezuma, and almost on queue, there was drumming. "Come on, really, here in New Mexico!" But then I remembered, New Mexico had been part of his empire also. Most of the US may have been for that matter. Now I heard flutes, flutes! I'd never heard those before, had I? A bright light suddenly exploded in my consciousness and there sitting upon his resplendent throne sat the emperor of all the Aztecs of Aztlán, Moctezuma the Magnificent, tormentor and owner of my lower intestine. He was now surrounded by beautiful nubile Mexican virgins and birds of every color of the rainbow flying in every direction. It was quite a sight. Funny thing is, he just sat there staring at me, that's all.

The birds continued to perform aerial acrobatics around the emperor. The virgins lounged around his majesty's stead, dressed in all the feathers of creation. But old Moctezuma just continued to stare at me.

Finally realizing my nemesis was in expectation of some kind of response on my part, I said, "Okay, you had your fun with me through my physical misery for now over three weeks. There hasn't been a single moment when I have felt safe to relax for fear of you forming a counterattack. Not a moment's complete rest have you allowed me. Never!" At that moment it suddenly occurred to me I was talking to a hysterical illusion created by my own mind. But if none of this was real, why was he still staring at me?

Relenting to my subconscious need to project the Emperor Moctezuma in an unfading luminescence, I resolved to tell this phantasm a piece of my mind. But that's not what happened though, instead I remembered our journey and how much we had experienced traveling Moctezuma's great empire. We had visited a multicultural nation of native locals who comprise the heart and soul of Mexico. We had crossed rivers and jungles, swam in oceans, even crossed living volcanoes smoking gently into the atmosphere. The ancient ruins we had seen and climbed gave us an insight into how intimidated the conquistadors had to have been in their first encounter with this new civilization which had at the time, far surpassed anything Europe had to offer. At this point in their encounters, Moctezuma ruled one of the most sophisticated and advanced societies in the world. There truly was no one to compare him to.

With all these thoughts flowing through my mind in flashes of enlightenment, I became aware of what a gift I had been allowed. My old buddy, Moctezuma, had been a reminder to me of what a struggle Mexico had evolved from. Pain in that struggle was simply a part of what change demanded to birth a new nation. I think I had it now. My plumed teacher had somehow gotten through to me. There was more to the journey than simply transporting ourselves through a foreign land, much more.

With this new insight to his constant appearances through my consciousness the last three weeks, a sense of gratitude suddenly overwhelmed me. This whole uncomfortable extended experience had actually been a gift. Moctezuma continued to stare at me. Since he was in my mind I couldn't bow to him, but I could speak to him. With that I said, "Thank you for everything and everyone who comprises the great nation of Mexico, past and present. You were a great emperor and did not deserve Hernan Cortez."

He smiled at this. The first smile he ever exhibited to me. It was a good smile. Then he rose from his throne, stood stock still, and said, "*De Nada*" (You're welcome).

I said, "What, Spanish, you speak Spanish, what ta' hell! All that time I was suffering we could have communicated."

He turned to go with the virgins following.

"Wait a minute," I said, "I want to talk to you."

Totally oblivious, he simply strolled away with his entourage into a jungle mist. The last one trailing him was a quite attractive virgin in blue feathers. She turned to me at the very last moment, smiled, and winked at me, winked! Then, she too was gone.

What was that all about? Who knows, but I felt the curtains falling, and this performance of my imagination coming to an end. The usher of my dream led me out of the theater and into my transport to dreamland, and that was that.

EPILOGUE
"THE CIRCUS OF CALIGULA"
OCTOBER 1975

Upon returning to school for the new semester at our new campus, I was approached by the powers that be about the assembly presentation of our trip to Mexico. I kindly explained we had lost the travel diaries, due to a car break in. The fact that most of our film and cameras being stolen didn't help the situation at all either. I presented the principal, Bill Rada, with the reality of the debacle of elements this presented to an appropriate presentation. To this, Bill inquired, "You lost all the film?"

Thinking quickly, I responded, "Well, Bill, I did find three rolls of slide film in my suitcase, but I have no idea what the students shot."

Bill responded, "At least that's something, and the whole school wants to know what your adventure to the country south of us had to offer eight Navajos in experiences and insights."

I told Bill I had no notes because they were stolen, and the route that our expedition traveled remained the only thing still fresh in my mind.

Bill said patiently, "Let's do this, and you can show what slides you have, and you can narrate a semblance of a journey's trek across Mexico. At least that will be something, and the kids will love it."

Bill Rada was a freshly minted principal for the high school at Pine Hill, our spanking new school. He had been a journalism teacher, but somehow, he had gotten promoted over the summer. Well, good for him.

Any who, I agreed to this and started planning the presentation. No big deal—slide projector was in the new gym, and students would be lined up on the bleachers. Piece of cake. All I had to do was go to Brooks, film developers in Albuquerque, and get the slides developed from the trip, and Wa La! From there I would grab my trusty Mexico map and write an outline of our past itinerary. It wouldn't be a lot, but it at least would prove that we had left the state in the first place.

The planned assembly was for the middle of October. At the end of the first week of the month, I had returned to Brooks to pick up the slides from the trip. Upon paying for the development, I moved to a light table, available to customers, and sorted out the images. "No, no, no, oh no!" Please tell me this was a bad dream. The slides, in essence, recorded any *cerveza* (beer) billboard we passed on the road throughout the country of Mexico. Secondly, our fine tribe of Navajo gentlemen had recorded the rear ends of every cute *senorita* (young woman) they came across. Half of the seventy-two images these young Turks had recorded were of a female landscape, in nature, rather than the beautiful natural surroundings we had been fortunate enough to observe. For some unexplainable happenstance, there were three images of the pyramids of Teotihuacan outside of Mexico City. That was what I had to work with—three pictures of the Sun and Moon pyramids, oh boy.

Returning to school, I explained my predicament to Bill.

He acknowledged my situation but informed me, "The show must go on, and besides everything has already been scheduled."

For some reason, I believe I detected a small amount of glee escaping from his shifting, squinting eyes. Maybe, he was anticipating another form of entertainment supplied at my expense. You devil, Bill.

The day of the school assembly occurred like a last day on death row for me. My time was running out and soon my real hanging, that I would not escape. I was finished and needed to accept my fate. Goodbye, cruel world. When all the students and faculty were finally seated, and the snickering and coughing somewhat abated, I turned on the slide projector, which shot onto a large portable screen at the end of the gym. Then I called for the lights to be lowered.

Now by the time this point in reality kicked in, I had previously done a psychological analysis of what had gone wrong with the initial planning for the students' recording of our adventure. Never once had I told them to take shots of specific subjects, be they archaeological or historical architecture, or vast landscapes we had viewed in our travels. I had just assumed that these things would interest them as it would me. "Oh, to be such a fool." These were young, virile, Navajo boys in high school, high school! Their aesthetics were radically averse to mine. They were looking for chicks and beer, I was looking for culture. Their interests were right where they should be at this stage in their life. I, on the other hand, had never considered this fact of life and missed the boat completely. So here I was, washed up in a school assembly, tap dancing my way through this performance.

I set up the three pyramid slides first and explained as much historical background to Teotihuacan as I would expect a school assembly could stand. And then I started rolling through my death sentence with the rest of the slides. One by one, I slowly projected the images onto the large screen. I thought, I was a dead man, but instead I heard laughter, giggling, and shouting in Navajo. Each individual image brought the entire audience to an eruptive laughing hysteria. What was going on? Well, I didn't expect this!

Eventually all seventy-two slides had completed their journey around the carousel, and the lights in the gym returned. I sat by the projector horrified and mortified in my shame. Funny thing was some of the students stopped by to pat me on the back. Was it a final farewell? Gathering up my useless notes and the slide carousel, I walked a death march back to my classroom. I spoke to no one. What would my next employment be, I wondered. Trash man?

Later in the day, other teachers just laughed out loud when I neared them. Bill eventually caught me in the office and said, "Well, that was entertaining."

Nothing else was said. After that, the day went by like any other. I thought to myself, "I'm alive, I still have a job and somehow almost everyone was actually entertained by the absurdity of it all. Was that luck or what?"

The remaining two years of my career as an art teacher at the Pine Hill High School, until I moved to Albuquerque to a full-time dream as an artist, presented a constant approach by younger students who asked me the same question eternally, "Hey, Shows, when you taking us to Mexico next?"

VIVA MEXICO!

AUTHOR'S NOTE

Memory is a funny thing. One person recalls clearly the events of an occurrence, and yet in opposition, another individual would argue the accuracy of the self-same story. It would seem each one of us takes a picture of the same actual event but at a different angle. As a result, no two views could ever be identical, and this is probably as it should be.

This story of Mexico, and the characters involved, follows closely only one of these individual's perspectives, mine, the teacher of the group. Much has gone into fishing for the details of our extraordinary adventure. With luck and a prayer for the accuracy of the past recollections involved, may I do it justice and hopefully bring a smile and maybe even a guffaw to you, my reader. Happy trails!

READERS GUIDE

1. Why did the author think it was important to take Navajo students for a journey through Mexico?

2. Could the author proceed today with the same travel as he did in 1975?

3. What would the author do today without travelers' checks?

4. Could anyone recreate today the same travel plan as was done in 1975?

5. Would the legal liabilities in this day and age permit such an adventure?

6. Why do you think the author took Chee Dodge Martin suspecting there would be problems?

7. How were the students natural swimmers when there was no access to bodies of water on the reservation?

8. How do you think the students felt about experiencing the Pacific Ocean and then the Gulf of Mexico after an overnight drive through the jungle?

9. How do you think students dealt with the concept of a different currency and interacting with a foreign culture after experiencing the solitary life of the reservation?

10. Did the author really feel rats nipping at his feet while hanging in the recesses of the Mexico City sewers from an open manhole?

11. How do you think the students felt standing atop a pyramid in Teotihuacan for the first time?

12. Do you think the author should have continued on after the barber incident in Merida instead of forsaking a further journey east?

13. Why did the author assume students would take photos of historic and cultural sites on their own? Was the author naïve to their lack of experiences coming from reservation life?

14. Why wasn't the author fired from teaching for letting students have alcohol at a party?

15. Was the author too young for the responsibility of an adventure with students at this time, and who would have, at any age, wanted that responsibility to begin with?

16. What was Moctezuma doing in this adventure in the first place?

17. Was Moctezuma a form of comic relief to exasperate the unexpected circumstances that were inescapable?

18. Would these students remember fondly the experiences of this 1975 adventure and ever marvel at the fact that their crazy teacher brought them back alive after all?

www.ingramcontent.com/pod-product-compliance
Lightning Source LLC
Chambersburg PA
CBHW051051230426
43666CB00012B/2649